YORK NOTES

General Editors: Professor A.N. Jeffares (*University of Stirling*) & Professor Suheil Bushrui (*American University of Beirut*)

Henry James

WASHINGTON SQUARE

Notes by Ian Richards

BA (CANTERBURY) MA (LONDON)

LONGMAN
YORK PRESS

YORK PRESS
Immeuble Esseily, Place Riad Solh, Beirut.

LONGMAN GROUP LIMITED
Longman House,
Burnt Mill,
Harlow,
Essex

First published 1984
ISBN 0 582 79214 2
Printed in Hong Kong by
Wilture Printing Co Ltd.

Contents

Part 1

Introduction

The life of Henry James

Henry James was born in New York in 1843. His grandfather had been an Irish immigrant who made three million dollars in business. His father, Henry James senior, had declined to enter the family business, preferring to study theology. He became an exponent of the philosopher Emanuel Swedenborg (1688–1772) and was a friend of Ralph Waldo Emerson (1803–82), Henry David Thoreau (1817–62) and Thomas Carlyle (1795–1881). Henry James was the second of his five children. The elder brother, William James (1842–1910), became a well-known philosopher and psychologist, and a sister, Alice James (1848–92), wrote a famous journal, published posthumously.

Almost immediately after Henry's birth his parents took him to Europe for two years so that his cosmopolitan upbringing began very early. From 1855 onwards he was educated in Switzerland, England and France. In 1860 he returned to America to study art for a time in the studio of William Morris Hunt (1824–79). He was making his first youthful attempts at writing by this time and his father noted 'Harry is not so fond of study, properly so-called, as of reading. He is a devourer of libraries and an immense writer of novels and dramas'. An injury to his back kept James from enlisting in the American civil war but his younger brothers, Wilkinson and Robertson James, fought for the triumphant Union army. James attempted to study law at Harvard from 1862 to 1863 but gave it up. By now he wanted to be a man of letters. His first tale, *The Story of a Year*, appeared in *The Atlantic Monthly* in 1865, but he felt that America regarded a writer's profession as too unbusinesslike to be acceptable. The young James also felt himself to be alienated from the world about him, always observing people and places as if from the outside. This sense of critical, ironic detachment was to remain with him all his life. He turned it to great advantage in his novels, and it is one of the features of his fictional style.

From 1865 James continued to publish tales and criticism (the critical work James produced during his life-time became highly influential) and in 1869 he made his first unaccompanied trip to Europe. He spent most of his time there in Italy, which captivated him, but visited also England, France and Switzerland. While in England he heard of the death of his cousin, Mary ('Minnie') Temple, of tuberculosis at twenty-four. She was a highly attractive and intelligent young woman and James seems to have been in love with her. He never declared his feelings to her, as she was surrounded by other admirers, but she became the model for many of his heroines, such as Isabel Archer in *The Portrait of a Lady* and Mildred Theale in *The Wings of a Dove*. Perhaps because of her early death he never married.

James returned to his parents' new home in Cambridge, Massachusetts, in 1870, but in 1872 went to Europe once more. He wanted to write about people's customs, manners and habits and to place them within an artistic framework or 'form'. He felt America offered less opportunity for form than he wished, because it was such a young country. It was in the richer culture of Europe that he felt most comfortable, and many of his novels explore the theme of the meeting of American and European cultures and values and are set in both continents. It has also been suggested by James's biographer, Leon Edel, that James felt overshadowed by the presence of his brother William and that this aroused in him a desire to escape. William could be highly critical of his younger brother, which James felt keenly, and he seems to have suffered from feelings of inferiority to his brother all his life. In 1874 he returned to New York and began publishing his impressions of the Old World in magazines. In the next year his second novel, *Roderick Hudson*, was serialised and he published a collection of short stories, *The Passionate Pilgrim*. These were well received.

James then left for Paris once more where he met the writers Ivan Turgenev (1818–83), Gustave Flaubert (1825–80), Edmond de Goncourt (1822–96), Ernest Renan (1823–92), Guy de Maupassant (1850–93), Alphonse Daudet (1840–97) and Emile Zola (1840–1902). Flaubert was the most influential in the group, having published his famous novel *Madame Bovary* some twenty years before. These men argued that an author's chief concern was the aesthetics of his work rather than the moral prejudices of his readers. Art should impress through the beauty of its technique, not simply through the quality of the values it embodied. This emphasis on form rather than content appealed to James. The call was for an art form in which things would be revealed and shown rather than merely talked of and commented on. The author should keep his personal opinions out of his work. This emphasis on objectivity was to become the basis of James's own aesthetic theories. But James still felt drawn to the spiritual largeness of the English novel and, finding English society friendly and hospitable, he settled in London in 1876. He published his third novel, *The American*, the following year.

England was to become James's home for life. It was here, in 1878, that he wrote his next novel, *The Europeans*, published his first book of criticism, *French Poets and Novelists*, and had the first novel he had written, *Watch and Ward*, published in book form. James soon found himself accepted by London society and after writing all day he would invariably dine out. He claimed to have accepted 140 invitations in the winter of 1878 alone. He liked the English and was liked by them, and although at times he thought them intellectually dull he also found them a rich subject for a novelist. Over the next decades he met many of England's best writers, including Alfred, Lord Tennyson (1809–92), George Eliot (1819–80), Robert Browning (1812–89), John Ruskin (1819–1900), Leslie Stephen (1832–1904), Mathew Arnold (1822–88), Robert Louis Stevenson (1850–94), Max Beerbohm (1872–1956), Joseph Conrad (1857–1924), Virginia Woolf (1882–1941) and Ford Madox Ford (1873–1939). James was to become an acknowledged master of his profession. At this time he wrote *Daisy Miller* in 1879, *Washington Square* in 1880 and *The Portrait of a Lady* in 1881.

Although his novels were well received by critics and magazines and book publishers continued to accept his works, James found that his popularity was falling and his books were not selling well. He began to get into financial difficulties which he held off only by his huge output. His father died in 1882, causing him to visit America briefly. His next three novels, *The Bostonians*, *The Princess Casamassima* and *The Tragic Muse*, although they have become classics, were complete commercial failures. A young Englishman, Edward Compton (1854–1918), had staged a dramatisation by James of *The American* in 1891, changing the ending to a happy one, and had made a small profit. James now determined to write for the theatre. He wrote four plays that did not reach production but *Guy Domville* was staged in London in 1895. The play ran for only one month and although it was given favourable reviews by Shaw, Wells and Arnold Bennett (1867–1931), it was another failure. James was even jeered when he appeared to take the curtain call on the first night. James's dialogue was too stiff and literary to be successful on the stage and this has always been one of his limitations. Even in his novels James's characters all speak in the same manner, although here this may be justified as serving to preserve a stylistic unity between the narrative and the dialogue.

James turned back to fiction. He now wrote a series of novels in an increasingly elaborate style, combining a more and more difficult syntax with increased use of colloquialisms and metaphors. The results were *The Spoils of Poynton* and *What Maisie Knew* in 1897, *The Awkward Age* in 1899, *The Sacred Fount* in 1901, *The Wings of a Dove* in 1902, *The Ambassadors* in 1903, *The Golden Bowl* in 1904 and a string of very fine short stories or tales including *The Aspern Papers*, *The Turn of the Screw* and *The Beast in the Jungle*. In 1898 James moved to Lamb House at Rye in Sussex, but kept in touch with London society by means of letters and telegrams.

Then in 1905 James returned to America, which he had not visited for twenty years, to lecture and see his brother William and family. He wrote down his impressions of the new world he was rediscovering in *The American Scene* (1907) which proved very popular. There also appeared in the same year the definitive New York Edition of his literary works, together with prefaces by James on the difficulties he had faced in writing them. These prefaces remain a superb exposition of literary technique.

In 1910 James's brother William died, and in 1914 the first world war began. James's shock at the outbreak of hostilities seemed to prevent him from finishing his last two novels, *The Ivory Tower* and *The Sense of the Past*, although they were published posthumously. With the war the society James had observed and chronicled was to disappear and the period we know as 'modern' truly to begin. James did much valuable practical work at this time, aiding Belgian refugees, visiting hospitals and writing for war charities. He also realised how deep his love for England was and became a naturalised British subject. In December 1915 he suffered a stroke and remained an invalid until his death three months later, on 28 February 1916. He had been awarded the Order of Merit only shortly beforehand, the third novelist ever to receive this honour.

The origin of *Washington Square*

The idea for *Washington Square* was first suggested to James by a friend of his, the actress Fanny Kemble (1809–92). She told him that her brother had once been engaged to a dull girl who was to inherit a fortune from her father. The young man was interested in the girl only for the money and when the father threatened to disinherit her if she married Kemble the young man jilted her. The father died, the girl inherited her money, and ten years later Kemble returned to England again from his travels. He visited the young woman but she sent him away, although she never married anyone else.

James set the tale in New York and intended to write it as a short story. However it grew longer and longer to become not just a melodramatic story of a young girl's betrayal by the faithless man she loves but a complex psychological novel of her relationship with a well-meaning but tyrannical father and an over-romantic, fickle aunt. It was written in London in 1880 and serialised simultaneously by the *Cornhill Magazine* in England and by *Harper's New Monthly Magazine* in America during the same year. It was the first time ever that James's work appeared simultaneously in both countries. The profits from the book allowed him the leisure in which to write his next novel, *The Portrait of a Lady* (1881). Many regard this next book as his finest work, and certainly this was the period in his life in which he established himself as a major author. James himself was later dissatisfied with *Washington Square*, feeling that it was too simple and thin a narrative. But the public had disagreed, since *Washington Square* has always been one of the most popular of James's novels and critics have called it a small masterpiece.

A note on the text

The history of all Henry James's texts is extremely complex. James revised most of his works in 1905 for a collected edition published by Scribners of New York and now known as the New York Edition. Although this has become one of the standard editions for James's novels it excluded *Washington Square*, presumably because of James's dissatisfaction with it. Thus the text of the novel remains mostly unaltered. Following its first appearance in serial form in *Cornhill Magazine* (June–November 1880) with illustrations by George du Maurier, and in *Harper's New Monthly Magazine* (July–December 1880), *Washington Square* was published in one volume by Macmillan, London, in 1881. The commonly available text published by Penguin Books, Harmondsworth, 1963, is based upon the Macmillan edition and has been used in the preparation of these Notes.

Part 2

Summaries

of WASHINGTON SQUARE

A general summary

Catherine Sloper, a plain and rather ordinary girl who is likely to inherit a large sum of money on the death of her father, has started to receive attentions from a handsome young suitor, Morris Townsend. Her father, Dr Sloper, begins to taunt her with this, suspecting the motives of the young man who seems to have neither money of his own nor employment. Dr Sloper makes inquiries and finds his suspicions are correct. When Catherine tells him that Morris Townsend has proposed marriage to her and that she has accepted, her father tells her that she does not have his consent. If she goes ahead and marries Townsend she will forfeit her inheritance. Her aunt, Mrs Penniman, urges her to marry Townsend in secret, but Catherine loves her father as much as she loves her suitor and so waits patiently in the hope that Dr Sloper will change his mind. But Dr Sloper continues to taunt her. Eventually she agrees to marry Townsend in secret, but he now advises her to wait, because he privately wishes to make sure of the inheritance. At last Dr Sloper takes Catherine on a voyage to Europe, hoping that Townsend will give her up and she will forget him. Her father continues constantly to abuse her during their European tour and Catherine returns more determined to marry Townsend than before. But her lover is worried that Dr Sloper is still refusing to give his consent. Townsend says that he cannot bear to have her give up her life of luxury for one of poverty with him. Catherine, now embittered and alienated from Dr Sloper, sees that Townsend is lying and does not really love her. Her heart is broken but she tells her father the engagement is over and endures her grief. Dr Sloper, now haunted by the fear that Catherine will marry Townsend on his death, tries to make his daughter promise that she will never marry him. Catherine refuses and before the doctor dies he alters his will, greatly reducing his daughter's inheritance. Years later Townsend, now a widower, reappears and, aided by Mrs Penniman, proposes again to Catherine, thinking that her small inheritance is better than nothing. But Catherine, who has never married or moved from Washington Square, is now capable of seeing through him and refuses him.

Detailed summaries

Chapter 1

The novel opens with a description of the medical profession in New York and of Dr Sloper as a respected member of it. He has been a successful and clever doctor, happily married and wealthy. But his happiness is ruined by the deaths first of his infant son and then of his wife when she gives birth to a second child, Catherine. Resigned, Dr Sloper resolves to make the best of his daughter.

NOTES AND GLOSSARY:

The first half of the present century: that is 1800–50

This profession in America: James begins with the general and moves quickly in the second paragraph to the particular, that is, to Dr Sloper's character and life history

the grassy waysides of Canal Street: James has a keen sense of place, and draws a very convincing picture of old New York with little touches such as this

Chapter 2

Catherine is brought up by her widowed aunt, Lavinia Penniman, and her father. Mrs Penniman is the less favourite of Dr Sloper's two sisters, an over-romantic, shallow, selfish woman who comes to visit the doctor and remains to stay as a permanent house-guest. Catherine grows into a healthy young girl with no special qualities of intelligence, reason or force of personality for her father to admire. He hides his disappointment of her, expecting nothing, while she hides her kind heart and gentle nature behind her shyness.

NOTES AND GLOSSARY:

Poughkeepsie: at this time a small town outside New York

the poor motherless girl should have a brilliant woman near her: a fine example of James's irony since Mrs Penniman is obviously not brilliant

You are good for nothing unless you are clever: Dr Sloper has a bias towards the intellect and intellectual pursuits. He regards intelligence as quite superior to any good nature that Catherine might have

Lavinia will try and persuade her that some young man...: this thought is prophetic, but also determines the doctor's own thinking when the situation actually occurs, so that he underestimates the depth of Catherine's feelings

you would have found her lurking in the background: Catherine is unconventional material for a heroine because, like most of us, she is an ordinary person. But in the last sentence of the chapter James shows that he is on her side

Chapter 3

Catherine becomes a young lady with a taste for expensive dresses, and although she has only a small allowance and must curb her desires, she will one day inherit a large fortune from her father. As New York expands and commerce takes over the area in which they live, the Slopers move to Washington Square. Catherine becomes a regular visitor to the house of her aunt, Mrs Almond, and her nine cousins.

NOTES AND GLOSSARY:

up town: farther away from the centre of the city and closer to the suburban areas

Washington Square: located at the bottom of Fifth Avenue, Washington Square is a small park now in the heart of fashionably residential Greenwich Village. Washington Place, where James was born, is near by, and, even at the time of James's writing in 1880, Washington Square would no longer have been the quiet new neighbourhood it was in 1835. The famous reminiscing that follows must surely be James recalling his own childhood, and it stands out in a novel written with such economy of style

Chapter 4

At the engagement party of one of her cousins Catherine is introduced to Morris Townsend who has recently returned to New York from abroad. He pays much attention to Catherine who is captivated by his charm, wit and physical beauty. They talk and she learns that he is related to the fiancé of Marian Almond. Later Catherine sees Morris Townsend engaged in conversation with her aunt Penniman who also seems to approve of him. Going home from the party in their carriage Dr Sloper asks Mrs Penniman about this young man and says that he must be interested in Catherine's money. Both Mrs Penniman and Catherine defend Townsend's motives.

NOTES AND GLOSSARY:

a very big sash: a reference to the fashions of the time

the harmonious rotation of the polka: the polka was a quick dance

It was very kind of Catherine to take pity on him: an example of James's stylistic subtlety. The preceding sentences in the paragraph give Catherine's point of view, showing her perceptions of Morris Townsend. The remainder of the paragraph following this sentence reproduces indirectly Townsend's words, so completely does his presence dominate Catherine's mind

dissembling for the first time in her life: we can see the influence of Townsend on Catherine is not entirely good, and it is significant that she goes on to lie to her father

Who was that young man that was making love to you?: 'making love to' meant at this time 'talking and paying attention to'

Chapter 5

Morris Townsend and his cousin Arthur pay a social visit to Washington Square. While Morris is conversing with Mrs Penniman Catherine learns from his cousin that Morris has no employment. When the callers have gone Mrs Penniman tells Catherine that Morris Townsend has come to court her, and Catherine feels that this is almost too good to be true.

NOTES AND GLOSSARY:

Excelsior!: a popular poem by Henry Wadsworth Longfellow (1807–82)

Some place or other; some business: we have already learnt in Chapter 1 that in order to be respectable in New York a man must have employment

She was incapable of elaborate artifice: Catherine's innocence puts her at a disadvantage when surrounded by sophisticated people

he is coming a-courting: meaning that Townsend has marriage in mind

---

Chapter 6

Morris Townsend calls again and this time Catherine sees him alone, utterly charmed by his light, easy speech. Dr Sloper hears of the visit and, suspicious that the suitor is after his daughter's inheritance, speaks sarcastically of him to Catherine. He then approaches his sister, Mrs Almond, for information about the young man. She tells him Mrs Penniman has already seen her for the same reason. She then says that Townsend does not come from a respectable branch of the Townsend family, has spent his small inheritance while travelling abroad and is at present living upon the income of his own sister, Mrs Montgomery. The doctor resolves to visit Mrs Montgomery.

NOTES AND GLOSSARY:

the young man's name was brought in: in those days wealthy people had servants who met visitors at the door, told those in the house who was calling, and conducted the visitors to the drawing-room

He had omitted, by accident, to say that he would sing to her if she would play to him: this calculating behaviour is not at all natural and throws doubt upon Townsend's motives for seeing Catherine

she has a style of her own: Mrs Almond's favourable judgment of Catherine shows that Catherine has personal qualities after all that suggest she is a worthy heroine

Chapter 7

Meanwhile Dr Sloper, not wanting to be too hasty in his judgment, invites Townsend to dinner. They meet, and although the doctor is impressed by the young man's good looks and intelligence he does not like him, thinking him too insinuating and familiar. Townsend tells Catherine of this, and she says her father's opinion matters. It is Mrs Penniman who says his opinion is not important.

NOTES AND GLOSSARY:

something of a physiognomist: someone who can guess the character of a person from the features of their body or face

a gleam of fine impatience in the social softness of his eye: once again we see that Townsend is not as pleasant as he is pretending to be

a plausible coxcomb: a vain and foolish person who is capable of tricking people into believing him to be worthy of respect

Chapter 8

Catherine is afraid to mention Morris Townsend to her father and Townsend continues to visit Washington Square during the day while Dr Sloper is at work. Eventually Dr Sloper asks Mrs Penniman for information. She seems to be completely charmed by Townsend and says that although he has had a disreputable past he now repents it and that his interest in Catherine is sincere. The doctor declares he is certain that Townsend is after Catherine's money, and they argue.

NOTES AND GLOSSARY:

Deeply sincere: Mrs Penniman's conviction that Morris Townsend is honourable goes against what we already suspect, and suggests that she has been taken in by his charm

if you regard Catherine as a weak-minded woman: later events show that while Catherine may be mistaken about Townsend's sincerity she is too stubborn to be weak-minded

---

Chapter 9

At a Sunday evening family gathering at Mrs Almond's house Dr Sloper, Morris Townsend and Catherine meet once again. In an effort not to judge Townsend too harshly Dr Sloper questions the young man about his lack of employment. Townsend replies that he is a tutor to his aunt's *sisters* children, and Dr Sloper resolves once more to visit the young man's aunt. *sister* Townsend then tells Catherine that her father has insulted him over his poverty, and asks if they may meet outside her house in the Square gardens. He has something very important to tell her. But she demands that they meet at her house, much to Mrs Penniman's disappointment.

NOTES AND GLOSSARY:

poetic justice: the ideal situation in which people get exactly what they deserve in return for their actions

She rather depends on me, you see: we, and the doctor, know that this is a lie and that he lives on his sister

I am not even brave: yet Catherine is firm enough to force Townsend to do what she chooses: they will meet in her house —as was socially correct in the nineteenth century

---

Chapter 10

Morris Townsend comes to Washington Square again and declares his love to Catherine. She accepts his declaration and says that they must speak to her father. She will speak to him first tomorrow and Townsend will speak to him afterwards. Townsend warns Catherine that Dr Sloper will say he is after her money and Catherine says she will tell the doctor that he is mistaken. She promises Townsend to stand by him and be faithful to him if her father is against the marriage.

NOTES AND GLOSSARY:

she took what was given her from day to day: until now Catherine has passively accepted Townsend's attentions and would not have been heartbroken if they stopped. But with her promises to be faithful in this chapter

	she commits herself to loving him and becomes in her eyes forever united with him
you are of age:	old enough to marry without her father's consent

Chapter 11

Catherine tells her father that she is engaged to Morris Townsend. Dr Sloper, who is expecting such a conversation, says that Townsend should have spoken first, that he himself has allowed Catherine much liberty for which she should be grateful, and that he dislikes the engagement. Catherine asks if this is because Townsend is mercenary, and the doctor says he wishes to avoid saying such things. But he goes on to give his reasons for disliking the engagement, namely that Townsend has squandered his own inheritance and is now too interested in Catherine's. Catherine attempts to defend her lover. Dr Sloper says that he will see Townsend the next day.

NOTES AND GLOSSARY:

he was determined to be very mild: another example of Dr Sloper making up his mind beforehand. He has already decided to disapprove of his daughter's relationship with Townsend

'Is it serious?' said the Doctor: an odd and humorous response to his daughter's announcement of her engagement. The doctor does not wish to take it seriously

You won't think me cruel?: a pointless question since this is precisely how Catherine feels

Chapter 12

Morris Townsend visits Dr Sloper and is told that the doctor disapproves of the engagement. Townsend asks if this is so because he is poor and the doctor agrees, saying that he lacks money, a profession, and prospects. Townsend offers his word as a gentleman that he is not mercenary but the doctor refuses to believe him. Townsend says that although he spent his own inheritance he would be more careful with Catherine's but the doctor refuses to believe this also. He will not forbid his daughter to see Townsend any more but says he will ask, and she will do as he asks. Townsend says that he and Catherine will continue to see each other and defy him.

NOTES AND GLOSSARY:

The word of a gentleman that I am not mercenary: Dr Sloper's first impression of Townsend in Chapter 7 was that he was not a gentleman

I am not a father in an old-fashioned novel: by making the characters conscious of the fairy-tale roles they assume, James heightens the realism in the book and keeps the characters from turning into fairy-tale stereotypes

Chapter 13

Dr Sloper's second sister, Mrs Almond, suggests that he may have been too hasty in judging Townsend. The doctor says that he will check his impressions by visiting Townsend's sister, Mrs Montgomery. Mrs Almond says that Mrs Montgomery is an exemplary woman and will tell him the truth. Dr Sloper mentions that Catherine is taking the news of his disapproval very quietly.

NOTES AND GLOSSARY:

a humbug: a hoax, fraud or an impostor

It makes ... the effort of choosing between you and her lover almost impossible: James is using Mrs Almond to state Catherine's dilemma plainly

Chapter 14

Dr Sloper visits Mrs Montgomery and they discuss Morris Townsend. The doctor says Catherine will inherit ten thousand dollars left to her by her mother but that if she marries Townsend he will leave another twenty thousand dollars of his own not to Catherine but to his nephews and nieces. Eventually he forces Mrs Montgomery to admit that Townsend is selfish and shallow, has taken money from her and lives at her expense. The doctor says that he will compensate her for the cost of keeping Townsend and she tells him not to let Townsend marry his daughter.

NOTES AND GLOSSARY:

baby-house: doll's house

the leafy season: summer

glossy poplin lap: poplin is a dress material, a mixture of silk and worsted

he teaches them—Spanish: the second most common language in the United States after English, but only a small part of a young gentlewoman's necessary upbringing

Chapter 15

Catherine surprises her father by taking Morris Townsend's banishment from Washington Square very quietly. She is, in fact, being remarkably patient and hoping that the situation will right itself. She writes to Townsend asking him to wait until she has made up her mind, and he writes in return that she cannot possibly mean to give him up. Meanwhile Mrs Penniman, foolishly hoping to unite Townsend and Catherine in some sort of clandestine marriage, calls Townsend to a secret meeting in an oyster saloon. He comes reluctantly to hear what she has to say.

NOTES AND GLOSSARY:

You must *act*, my dear: this is advice quite contrary to Catherine's nature, since it is always in her character to remain passive

duenna: a chaperon, a woman who watches over the interests of a young girl in her care

oyster saloon: low-class restaurant specialising in oyster dishes. Oysters are also widely regarded as an aphrodisiac

she went to the tryst at dusk: a tryst is a meeting of lovers. James is being ironic here, but also commenting on Mrs Penniman's attitude to the meeting

Chapter 16

Mrs Penniman tells Morris Townsend that Dr Sloper will never yield to argument and the best plan is for him to marry Catherine in secret. She says that by doing this Townsend would prove that he is not interested in Catherine's money, since Dr Sloper would disinherit her. But eventually Dr Sloper would let his daughter have the inheritance money anyway, out of a sense of duty. Townsend is tempted, but not convinced by the idea. He says he would not want to hurt Catherine by depriving her of her inheritance. He sends Catherine a message to hold fast, then walks Mrs Penniman back to Washington Square and parts with her there.

NOTES AND GLOSSARY:

a certain vagueness in her errand: in fact Mrs Penniman has met Townsend out of a fanciful desire to see him again, rather than an urge to help Catherine

Mrs Penniman always, even in conversation, italicized her personal pronouns: James shows us what an artificial person Mrs Penniman really is

Chapter 17

Mrs Penniman tells Catherine of her secret meeting with Morris Townsend, but Catherine does not feel this was right since she has promised her father not to see him. Mrs Penniman says that she has made no promises to Dr Sloper and tells Catherine that Morris Townsend said he was ready to marry her any day, in spite of everything. She says that Catherine is cold and asks if she is going to give Townsend up. She puts pressure on Catherine not to submit to her father. Catherine repeats that she does not like Mrs Penniman meeting Townsend in secret.

NOTES AND GLOSSARY:

He said he was ready to marry you any day, in spite of everything: this is a lie, since Townsend said no such thing. Instead it is what Mrs Penniman would like to imagine he said

I don't know what will become of us: by saying 'us' rather than 'you' Mrs Penniman betrays that she is really more concerned about herself than about Catherine

I don't think it is your place to teach me what is right: in fact Catherine's instincts as to what is right are far better than Mrs Penniman's

Chapter 18

The same night Catherine visits her father in his study and tells him that she would like to see Morris Townsend again. She says that she has already written to him four times and that she would like to see him to tell him to wait for her. Dr Sloper says that their waiting would make them long for his death, but Catherine says that she will never marry once her father is dead. She says she hopes Townsend will little by little change her father's opinion of him. Dr Sloper replies that he will never speak to Townsend again and that if Townsend marries her he will not leave her any of his money. Catherine is resolved to see her lover and her father says it will cause him great pain. Catherine bursts into tears and Dr Sloper sends her from the room.

NOTES AND GLOSSARY:

his study: a room used for reading and study

the parlour: a family living-room

an epigram: a short, sarcastic saying

I believe she will stick: the doctor believes that for a time at least Catherine will not give way and he is quite looking forward to the struggle, something he never thought he would get from his daughter

Chapter 19

Dr Sloper sees Mrs Penniman the next morning and warns her to be careful in siding with Morris Townsend and Catherine against him. Mrs Penniman accuses Dr Sloper of being tyrannical, says that Catherine passed the night weeping and that the doctor will lose her just as he lost his wife and son. The doctor becomes very angry and threatens Mrs Penniman with dismissal from his house if she crosses him. Mrs Penniman knows Catherine spent the night weeping because it was she who comforted the girl after Catherine left Dr Sloper's study. But next morning Mrs Penniman is most surprised to see Catherine up early for breakfast and not languishing in bed, as a heartbroken heroine should. Catherine says that her father would not like it and she has no special desire to offend him. Nevertheless her heart is breaking and so she summons Townsend to Washington Square to speak to him.

NOTES AND GLOSSARY:

she should mind her p's and q's: she should be careful how she acts

a fib: a lie

She had a most impracticable physique: James ironically implies that
                        Catherine's healthiness is not suited in Mrs Penni-
                        man's eyes to the role of suffering heroine

Chapter 20

Morris Townsend visits Washington Square and urges Catherine to marry him against her father's will. But Catherine wants to wait and see if her father will become reconciled to the idea. Townsend asks if this is possible and says that she is afraid of her father, which Catherine admits. She says that she is willing to wait a long time. She then delivers Dr Sloper's message that if she were to marry Morris Townsend she would not inherit a penny of the doctor's money. Townsend is convinced that if they are married the doctor will never forgive her, and just as he is asking if some cleverness on Catherine's part might bring Dr Sloper round she agrees to marry him in secret.

NOTES AND GLOSSARY:

Morris's luminosity seemed almost pitiless: this is Catherine's own
                        impression. Townsend treats her as selfishly as her
                        father

For your sake what am I not ready to face?: in fact Townsend is risking
                        nothing by courting Catherine, and has everything
                        to gain by it.

Chapter 21

Dr Sloper tells Mrs Almond with great enthusiasm that he believes Catherine will resist him over Townsend. Mrs Almond notes that the doctor is very cold-hearted, but agrees that Catherine will cling to her lover. Enjoying the challenge, Dr Sloper says he will take Catherine to Europe to make her forget Townsend. Meanwhile Mrs Penniman meets Townsend again. She advises him not to marry Catherine without her father's consent but to wait for him to come round. She says that if they were to marry she herself would be thrown out of Washington Square. Townsend is irritated by this because he says he has just convinced Catherine that she should marry him in secret, but Mrs Penniman points out that Catherine loves him so much that she would certainly not think the worse of him for postponing their marriage.

NOTES AND GLOSSARY:

a geometrical proposition: the formal statement of a theorem in geometry to be proved true, or in this case, the doctor's desire to prove himself right

I hope you have come to tell me that he has knocked under: to tell me that he has given in

I recommend you to take one way and stick to it: this is also what Dr Sloper thinks the lovers will do, and it is Mrs Penniman who breaks what all have imagined will be the likely pattern of events

he threatens, if anything happens, to turn me out of the house: Mrs Penniman tells Townsend this because she feels that concern for her will cause him to delay the marriage. In fact it is her other argument, that Catherine can be made to wait until her father changes his mind, that convinces Morris Townsend

Chapter 22

It seems that Morris Townsend has secretly decided to postpone his marriage to Catherine. He carefully avoids naming the day when it is to take place. Meanwhile Catherine is convinced the wedding will take place soon and tells her father that she will see Townsend once a week until they are married. Her father coldly replies that he does not care how often she sees Townsend, it is all against his wishes. He then asks her to put her marriage off for a few months, because he would like to take her to Europe with him for six months. Catherine, delighted at having an opportunity to show her respect for her father, agrees.

NOTES AND GLOSSARY:
the complete absence of revenue is nowhere counted as an advantage: James is now quite open in showing us Townsend's mercenary ideas
This striking argument gave the Doctor a sudden sense of having underestimated his daughter: for the first time Dr Sloper suspects that he will have trouble controlling Catherine

---

Chapter 23

After gaining Morris Townsend's approval, Catherine leaves for Europe with her father, even though she would rather have stayed behind with her suitor. They plan to marry on Catherine's return. Dr Sloper is so taken with the art and antiquities of Europe that he stays for twelve months rather than just six. Meanwhile Townsend often visits Mrs Penniman in Washington Square, smoking the doctor's cigars and enjoying the comfort of the house which was denied to him before. Mrs Penniman approves of all this.

NOTES AND GLOSSARY:
the ruins of the Pantheon: the ancient Roman temple of all the gods
there was a spark of anger in her grief: Catherine's way of thinking has changed and she is now beginning to suspect that she has been treated badly

---

Chapter 24

After they have been travelling together for six months Dr Sloper suddenly asks Catherine about Morris Townsend when they are walking alone together in the Alps. Catherine, a little afraid, replies that she has not given him up and that he writes to her twice a month. The doctor says he is very angry and that Townsend would leave her to starve in a situation just as cruel as these mountains, but Catherine vehemently defends her lover. The subject is not mentioned again for another six months, until the eve of their departure for America, when the doctor asks if Catherine will marry Townsend on her return. She replies yes and that he still writes to her often of the wedding. Dr Sloper asks her to give him three days' warning before he loses her to Townsend forever.

NOTES AND GLOSSARY:
the Alps: a mountain range separating France from Italy
the excitement of having for the first time spoken to him in violence: Catherine has now been forced to defy her father openly and there is pathos in her defending Townsend when we know his worthlessness

Liverpool: a port and city in the north-west of England frequently used as an embarkation port for America

Catherine at last took her candle to go to bed: before the use of electricity people took a lighted candle with them to find their way to their bedrooms at night

Chapter 25

On her return Catherine talks to Mrs Penniman who says that she has seen a lot of Morris Townsend in the past year. She tells Catherine that Townsend used to come to Washington Square often and sit in Dr Sloper's study, and Catherine is not pleased at this. But when she hears that Townsend has found employment by going into partnership with a commission merchant she is much happier although she knows it will not make any difference to her father. She tells Mrs Penniman that she is resolved to forget her inheritance and marry against Dr Sloper's wishes, and she is surprised when Mrs Penniman suggests that she should wait and try to win her father over. Catherine berates her for this. She says that a year ago Mrs Penniman was advising her to marry at once and that now she is determined to do so.

NOTES AND GLOSSARY:

your father's study: the room where Dr Sloper reads and works, and has his books and desk

a commission merchant: an agent who carries out business for others for a fixed percentage

transported for life: in the nineteenth century criminal offenders were punished by being transported to the remote colonies, especially Australia, and forced to work under extremely harsh conditions

Chapter 26

Morris Townsend visits Catherine now that she is back in Washington Square. They talk of Townsend's new employment and then Catherine says that Dr Sloper has not changed his mind and still opposes their marriage. Morris Townsend wants to try once more to speak to her father and persuade him. Catherine says firmly that this is impossible. She says that from talking to her father in Europe she knows that Dr Sloper is not very fond of her, that she feels separated from him and that she does not care about his disliking her lover. She adds that Townsend must be very kind to her because she has given up so much for him; he must never despise her as her father does. Morris Townsend promises this.

NOTES AND GLOSSARY:

there was a certain mild, sad firmness in her tone which he heard for the first time: confirmation of Catherine's new self-assurance on her return from Europe

He is not very fond of me: Catherine now feels totally cut off from her father and this makes her lean all the more heavily on Townsend

But for the moment he undertook nothing more onerous: Townsend promises to be kind to Catherine, but he carefully avoids promising to marry her since she has not got her father's consent

---

Chapter 27

Dr Sloper talks to Mrs Penniman and informs her that he is still as inflexible toward Morris Townsend as he was a year ago. Mrs Penniman sides with Townsend since she has now begun to regard him as if he were her own son. The doctor visits Mrs Almond. She tells him that Catherine says Townsend has set up a business and is making money. The doctor realises that Catherine has given him up, but this does not worry him. He says he wishes that she would change her mind but that it now seems too late.

NOTES AND GLOSSARY:

Elizabeth has told no tales: Mrs Almond, the doctor's other sister, has not revealed the nature of Townsend's visits; the doctor has guessed it for himself

an induction: the art of making a general rule from observing particular instances

bring a suit against you: prosecute you in a court of law

tables d'hôte: meals in a restaurant at a fixed price for the whole meal

---

Chapter 28

Mrs Penniman writes to Morris Townsend telling him of Dr Sloper's position and offering her support. She arranges a meeting between them to tell Townsend of her sympathy for him. But he cuts her short, saying that if the doctor will never yield and give Catherine her inheritance then he must give her up. He says he could never forgive himself for depriving Catherine of her rights by coming between her and her father. Mrs Penniman agrees, thinking that after all it would not do for a man like Morris Townsend to marry a woman without money, when he might easily find someone better. Townsend says he is giving up

Catherine for a wider career and asks Mrs Penniman to console Catherine when he breaks off with her, but Mrs Penniman seems only able to
offer him her repeated support.

NOTES AND GLOSSARY:

She was to do her duty, quite irrespective of Catherine: in this chapter
we follow the perverse logic of Mrs Penniman's
mind as she sides with Morris Townsend, and turns
more and more against Catherine

I am intensely anxious to see you: the letter that follows is remarkably
like a love-note in tone

a little reticule: a small handbag common among women at the
time

a wider career: since Townsend's office is so hard to find and he is
able to leave it during peak business hours it is
doubtful if he is seriously engaged in any business
at all

Chapter 29

Morris Townsend visits Catherine repeatedly without breaking off
with her. He finds that Mrs Penniman has been afraid to do anything
to soften the blow. Catherine trusts her lover completely, but at last
when the wedding is never mentioned she begins to wonder what is
wrong with him. Townsend announces that he must go off to New
Orleans for some time in order to make some money, and that Catherine may not come with him because of yellow fever in the area. She
says that she is no more likely to catch yellow fever than he, and that in
any case she still has all the money they need. Townsend argues, then
gives way and they argue about the day of his next visit. Catherine
suddenly realises that her lover is running away from her and tries to
prevent him leaving the room. She tells him he is leaving her; Townsend says he will write her a letter. Catherine says he will not come back;
he promises that he will.

NOTES AND GLOSSARY:

name the day: set a date for the wedding
New Orleans: a city far away in the southern part of the United
States
yellow fever: a contagious and often fatal disease

Chapter 30

Catherine gives way to her unhappiness, now that she is beginning to
see Morris Townsend in his true colours. She then pulls herself together

and for several days refuses to let either her father or Mrs Penniman know what has happened, even though both have guessed the engagement is over. Dr Sloper is pleased to have been proved right. Mrs Penniman, remembering that she has promised Morris Townsend to soften the blow, tries to approach Catherine to find out exactly what happened. Meanwhile Catherine has walked to Townsend's house, only to find that he has gone away. She asks her aunt where he can be and Mrs Penniman says that in view of their separation the farther away he goes the better. At mention of the word 'separation' Catherine realises that her aunt has been involved in Morris Townsend's actions. She blames her aunt for coming between them and asks if it was his plan to break off. Mrs Penniman agrees it was and says Morris Townsend could not bear to see her disinherited. Catherine sees that he has given her up and left her alone, but Mrs Penniman says that Catherine will still have her company.

NOTES AND GLOSSARY:

with an air of exaggerated courtesy, lifted his hat to her: a heartless thing for Dr Sloper to do, smugly to mock the conventions governing the relations between men and women, when he knows his daughter is suffering because of these

He couldn't bear to bring down on you your father's curse: this is only Townsend's excuse, but Mrs Penniman seems to believe it

Chapter 31

Mrs Penniman tells Mrs Almond that Catherine's engagement is off and that she is managing to console the girl. At the same time she advises Catherine not to let her father know that Townsend has backed out, and in fact this resolution not to give in to her father is all Catherine has left. She has received a letter from her suitor saying that he could not come between her and her fortune, that he will be away a long time, and that one day they will meet as friends. After a week Dr Sloper finds Catherine alone and asks her when she is going to be married and leave Washington Square. Catherine is forced to say that she has broken off the engagement and sent Morris Townsend to New York. Surprised, the doctor asks how he is taking it, and Catherine lets slip that she does not know.

NOTES AND GLOSSARY:

horsewhipped: the whip used to spur on horses was sometimes used on people as a severe and humiliating form of punishment in the nineteenth century and earlier

The Doctor had his revenge, after all: Dr Sloper's intellectual bias shows him more concerned with triumphing over his daughter than with comforting her

Chapter 32

As the years go by Dr Sloper remains unsure whether Catherine broke off with Morris Townsend or vice versa, and no one seems prepared to tell him. He does not talk to Mrs Penniman, and Mrs Almond, who has guessed the truth, will not tell him because she disapproves of his lack of sympathy for his daughter's suffering. As he grows older the doctor becomes more and more fearful that Townsend and Catherine are waiting patiently and in secret, to marry after his death. Catherine remains unmarried, despite two offers from other men, and slowly grows into a conservative, well-respected spinster devoted to charity and the young.

NOTES AND GLOSSARY:

abuse of sarcasm: at its most extreme irony becomes sarcasm (saying the exact opposite of what you mean in a hurtful way) and this is what Dr Sloper has been doing to Catherine

Chapter 33

One day Dr Sloper asks Catherine to promise that after his death she will not marry Morris Townsend. After all these years Catherine is surprised and her pride hurt that her father should expect her to promise this, and she refuses. The doctor says that in that case he will change his will. When later Dr Sloper dies his will is opened to find that he has not left all his money to Catherine, partly because she can live comfortably on her inheritance from her mother and partly to discourage Morris Townsend. He leaves most of his money to charities. Mrs Penniman is shocked by the will but Catherine is happy with it.

NOTES AND GLOSSARY:

the cicerone: any guide who helps tourists
the goatherd: someone who looks after herds of goats, then to be found in most parts of Europe
a codicil: an addition modifying a will

Chapter 34

Catherine and Mrs Penniman live on alone together in Washington Square. Eventually, twenty years after the engagement was broken off,

Mrs Penniman tells Catherine that she has seen Morris Townsend. He is back in New York, is much changed, and has failed to make his fortune. He married in Europe though his wife died soon after, and still retains his old charm. Mrs Penniman has told him that Catherine is unmarried and he would like to see her. Catherine stops Mrs Penniman from talking about her former lover and declares that she does not want to see him. To hear of him after all this time is a great shock to her and she quietly bursts into tears.

NOTES AND GLOSSARY:

warm evenings in July: in New York the height of summer

the fifth of a century: twenty years. James puts it this way to make it seem longer

a marriage of reason: this is the sort of marriage Townsend had hoped to make with Catherine

Chapter 35

A week later Mrs Penniman mentions Morris Townsend again. She delivers a message that he would like to see Catherine, to meet her as a friend. Catherine calmly refuses but at that moment the doorbell rings and Morris Townsend appears, invited by Mrs Penniman. Catherine recognises him, despite the changes of age, but feels that his old charm and winning manner are gone. She remains sure that it was wrong of him to call, and he becomes very embarrassed and asks her forgiveness. Catherine says she forgave him long ago; she does not hate him, but it would be impossible for them to be friends. Townsend implies that now the doctor is dead they are free to begin again, but Catherine calmly maintains that it was wrong of him to call, that she does not want his friendship. He leaves, and, meeting Mrs Penniman at the door, curses Catherine's dry manner. Catherine quietly takes up her embroidery again.

NOTES AND GLOSSARY:

fancy-work: ornamental embroidery, during the last century women's favourite evening occupation

It was the old voice, but it had not the old charm: if the voice is the same it must be Catherine, and her perceptions, which have changed

for life, as it were: this ending is often quoted as an example of pathos (something causing pity or sadness in the reader)

Part 3

Commentary

James's views on fiction

James and the craft of fiction

More than perhaps any other writer before or since James was a crafts-man. He believed that novels are not self-expressive bursts of the author's consciousness suddenly put down on paper but artefacts, care-fully ordered and put together. As a result he was always fascinated by literary technique and later in life published some of the most sustained pieces of critical work ever written on form in the novel (in the Prefaces that he added to the New York Edition of his books). In these he outlined his theories of fiction, many of which have greatly influenced the nature of what we value in modern literature.

Foremost in James's mind was the idea of impersonal narration. This technique, which was gaining ground at the time, was originally conceived by the French novelist Gustave Flaubert whom James met in Paris in 1875. It was felt that in too many novels in the past the author would often stop telling the story—that is, stop presenting the charac-ters' actions in a dramatic scene—and start giving in his own voice his views on how things were going in the book, whether he liked a particu-lar character or not, or his opinion about things entirely unrelated to the story. James, and others, believed that it was wrong for the author to intrude on his own narration and tell his readers what to think. Nar-ration should be impersonal, with nothing but the scene and characters presented, and the readers should be left to make up their own minds. Novels should not preach a moral code. Everything should be shown, nothing told. This resulted, they felt, in a more artistic novel in which aesthetic considerations and the craft of the novelist were the most important factor.

James was very concerned, then, in his novels with the presentation of dramatic scene. He felt that fiction was like a house with many win-dows for people to look through. People looking through different windows see the same thing, but see it from different angles and so in different ways. Therefore in *Washington Square* James enters the minds of many different characters, particularly of Catherine, Dr Sloper and Mrs Penniman, to show us their different opinions of what is happening, never James's own opinion. In this way we learn simultaneously about the scene and about the character who is viewing it. James is careful never to move into Morris Townsend's mind early in the novel because this would give away to us too much of the plot. He uses other means instead to indicate that Dr Sloper is right, which will be discussed later. This idea, that by looking at events from many different viewpoints we perceive them more truly, is vital in much modern writing and James helped to pioneer and promote it in his books.

The result, of course, of things being shown rather than told in novels is that much modern writing works by suggestion rather than by explanation and this often makes it very difficult to understand. It is not for nothing that the twentieth century has been the great age of literary criticism. Although James's voice may be heard at odd times in *Washington Square* it is never to give an opinion—he never gives us his opinion of Morris Townsend—but simply to state something already well known. 'Catherine, as I have said, sat up half the night' (Chapter 30). Instead of stating his views directly James often uses irony to put his own opinions across. Irony, the art of saying one thing when the reader knows you mean something else, is essentially an indirect way of stating your views. Often the reader needs to read very carefully to recognise it. When James says of Catherine 'her innocent arts were of little avail before a woman of the rare perspicacity of Mrs Penniman' (Chapter 30) we suspect irony because all previous evidence has suggested that Catherine is artless and Mrs Penniman not perspicacious. The result is an amusing stab at Mrs Penniman which suggests that the conclusions she is about to draw are wrong and also lets us know James's opinion of her as an imperceptive, stupid woman. Even more subtly, when Catherine prefers to receive Townsend's marriage proposal openly in her own parlour rather than secretly under the trees in the square, Mrs Penniman is told 'that her niece preferred, unromantically, an interview in a chintz-covered parlour to a sentimental tryst beside a fountain sheeted with dead leaves, and she was lost in wonderment at the oddity—almost the perversity—of the choice' (Chapter 9). It is, however, Mrs Penniman's sentimental tryst in the square that would be odd and would seem almost perverse, since it would not observe the proper nineteenth-century rules of conduct. At that time men proposed marriage to women in parlours and only met secretly in the open air for disreputable reasons. So James is telling us that it is Mrs Penniman who is odd and almost perverse in her disregard for what is right and proper, and that it is also disreputable of Morris Townsend to suggest such a thing in the first place.

James also uses characters such as Mrs Almond to suggest alternatives to the views of major characters. Mrs Almond in particular seems to carry special authority in her opinions and when she tells Dr Sloper of Catherine 'She won't forget him in Europe' (Chapter 21) we feel that she is probably correct. Mrs Almond contradicts Dr Sloper more and more often as the story progresses and we are made to feel that the doctor understands the action less and less clearly. In a novel as economic in the number of its characters as *Washington Square* the characters' opinions are often played off against each other, so that at the start of the novel we sympathise with Dr Sloper and by the end we are much more sympathetic to Catherine. Likewise, at the beginning of the novel, James's irony is often directed rather unsympathetically against Catherine, but, as the novel progresses, Catherine is described less and less ironically and it is Dr Sloper who is described ironically and unsympathetically.

Writing about America

When James began writing, America was still a very new country without a real sense of its own history, a country that still looked to Europe for its models of art and culture. This newness, writers felt, made America particularly poor material for literature because of its lack of usable rich traditions and past. The New York James writes about is not the metropolis of today but a small, though rapidly developing town on Manhattan Island which still has large areas of farmland. James wrote to a friend 'It takes an old civilisation to set a novel in motion—a proposition that seems to me so true as to be a truism. It is on manners, customs, usages, habits, forms, upon all these matured and established that a novelist lives—they are the very stuff that his work is made of'. For this reason James found it very difficult to write novels set wholly in America, and he felt this difficulty with *Washington Square*. He once described the novel as 'a tale purely American, the writing of which made me feel acutely the want of the [traditional] "paraphernalia"'.* Perhaps this is one reason why he never liked *Washington Square* much.

This newness of America is one of the reasons why James has Catherine go on a visit to Europe for one year during the novel. It is there that she acquires the inner strength and maturity that she needs in order to defy her father and eventually see through Morris Townsend. Even Dr Sloper recognises the effects of this European tour. He says 'I have done a mighty good thing for him [Morris Townsend] in taking you abroad; your value is twice as great, with all the knowledge and taste that you have acquired. A year ago, you were perhaps a little limited—a little rustic; but now you have seen everything, and appreciated

---

* Quoted from F.O. Mathiessen, *The American Novels and Stories of Henry James*, Alfred A. Knopf Inc., New York, 1947, p.xi.

everything, and you will be a most entertaining companion' (Chapter 24). It is still in Europe that people learn what is necessary to become worthwhile human beings, and the theme of Americans going to Europe to enlarge their capacity for life is a prominent one in all James's works.

It is to James's credit, then, that he has succeeded in setting so much of his novel in America, and attempted, though only with partial success, to give us a feeling of what New York and Washington Square must have been like in the nineteenth century. Novelists who write successful novels about their own country enrich the life of that country by giving certain features of it an extra, fictional significance. New York's real-life Washington Square is now 'Henry James territory' and, curiously enough, this provides the very paraphernalia necessary to later novelists.

The characters

Since *Washington Square* is a novel in which the background and 'paraphernalia' of the local New York culture are not very important, it seems likely that a high degree of emphasis is going to be placed on the characters. They will be doing more of the work of conveying the novel's meaning, and the conflict that is essential for all good novels and works of drama is likely to be centred on them rather than on their relationship to their background. James has very carefully kept the number of characters presented in the novel to a minimum in order to be able to show each of them in the greatest possible detail. But because James presents his characters without ever passing moral judgment upon them, because he—the author—never comes forward and tells us what to think, our interpretation of the characters can be very varied, and the way in which we judge them will determine the way in which we read the book. Is Dr Sloper heartlessly cruel, merely misguided or working in Catherine's best interests? Is Morris Townsend as unpleasant as Dr Sloper suspects? It is not until Chapter 5 in the novel at the earliest that we begin to suspect that Townsend is not the sincere admirer he appears to be and not until much later that this suspicion is confirmed. Since James's theory forbade him to tell his readers what to think, he focuses on the ordinary details of the characters' lives. His readers must form their ideas about the characters from these details.

Catherine Sloper

Catherine, says James, is 'the softest creature in the world' (Chapter 2). Named after her mother, who died giving birth to her, Catherine is Dr Sloper's second child (he had a son who died at three), a strong and healthy girl who is destined to inherit the sum of ten thousand dollars from her mother and a further twenty thousand dollars on the death of her father. A substantial fortune in those days, it is this twenty thousand dollars of his own that Dr Sloper threatens to withhold from his daughter. Catherine is a girl of small intelligence and limited imagination, and, as such, is a disappointment to her witty and intellectual father who sees these qualities as valuable. 'You are good for nothing unless you are clever' (Chapter 2), the doctor tells Mrs Penniman, and Catherine is not clever. Her nature is essentially passive and throughout the novel she allows things to happen to her rather than causes them to happen. Her resistance to her father is passive rather than active and her most decisive action is to refuse Morris Townsend upon his return at the end of the novel. She is extremely shy and quiet, and devoted to her father, although rather afraid of him. She is also fond of but not afraid of her aunt and is apparently unaware of Mrs Penniman's stupidity. She seems, then, poor material for the heroine of a novel.

There is, however, another side to Catherine's character, a side unnoticed by her father, of moral goodness and constancy. Catherine is an honest person, without social guile or ability to scheme, hence her obvious agitation on first being introduced to the handsome Morris Townsend and her naive admiration of his refinement. She lies to her father for the first time in her life when she declares to him that she does not know Morris Townsend's name, and she has no answer to her father's ironies. Catherine is a humble person. The only way she knows of expressing herself is indirectly, through her lively taste in dresses, but 'she had not a grain of coquetry, and her anxiety when she put them on was as to whether they, and not she, would look well' (Chapter 3). But Catherine is also a person who holds her opinions firmly. Mrs Almond says of her 'She doesn't take many impressions; but when she takes one, she keeps it. She is like a copper kettle that receives a dent. You may polish up the kettle but you can't efface the mark' (Chapter 21).

After her travels in Europe Catherine returns to Washington Square more self-assured and aware of her own worth. To Mrs Penniman she seems 'more mature' and 'rather handsome' (Chapter 25). She is capable of recognising her aunt's maliciousness and her father's ill-treatment of herself. Catherine's passivity has become a strength, an ability to suffer and endure in silence. She is willing to marry Morris Townsend, aware that he is unlikely to find employment and that in doing so she will lose two thirds of her inheritance. Since she has decided to give up all for him Townsend's cruel jilting of her destroys the basis of her life and thereafter she devotes herself, in her humanity, to philanthropic work. She never marries. 'The great facts of her career were that Morris Townsend had trifled with her affection, and that her father had broken its spring. . . . There was something dead in her life, and her duty was to try and fill the void' (Chapter 32). Catherine shows a stubborn integrity by remaining faithful to this sentiment and refusing such consolations as marriage to another and, finally, the world-weary Morris Townsend's offer of friendship at the novel's close.

Catherine is not a superficial person, yet most people in the novel judge her purely on the surface level. At the end of the novel she is forced by Mrs Penniman to meet Morris Townsend again and to refuse him, because Mrs Penniman is too shallow to see that Catherine is now emotionally exhausted and can see through her former lover. She is forced to acknowledge that the long years of her life have been wasted, and there is great pathos in her sitting down in the parlour at the novel's close 'for life, as it were' (Chapter 35).

Dr Sloper

Our interpretation of *Washington Square* will depend on the severity of our judgment of Dr Sloper. A grasp of the subtleties of his character is the key to understanding the book. He is a successful man, a highly competent doctor who married for love a woman of substantial income. He moves comfortably in the best New York society and is a man of keen intelligence and wit. Indeed his intellect has perhaps been developed at the expense of his emotions since it is through the power of his 'hard, intellectual nature' (Chapter 16) rather than through affection that he commands his daughter's respect. It is to his credit, though, that he is seldom wrong, and part of the book's tragedy is that he is not wrong about Morris Townsend.

One person, however, about whom his observation is not entirely correct is Catherine. After the death of his son and wife Catherine is all he has left in the world yet he treats her with detachment and regards her as a disappointment. His treatment of Catherine is in part a neurotic denial of the guilt he feels over his wife's death. His wife was the only woman he had ever met who had 'the beauty of reason' (Chapter 2) and he is disappointed that Catherine has not inherited this. He is so pleased to have Catherine's intellectual ordinariness confirmed that he fails to appreciate her good heart and moral worth. He decides to be philosophical, to accept his daughter's dullness and to 'expect nothing' (Chapter 2) from her. This detached view of his daughter means that later he regards her resistance to him as merely an interesting entertainment. Similarly he regards Mrs Penniman with contempt because she is 'a goose' (Chapter 2) and prefers his other sister, Mrs Almond, for her intelligence rather than her warmth.

Another aspect of the doctor's detached intelligence is his use of irony. We are told 'he almost never addressed his daughter save in the ironical form' (Chapter 4). In other words he never says to her what he means but only implies his meaning. Instead of telling Catherine that she is overdressed he says 'Is it possible that this magnificent person is my child?' (Chapter 4). This allows him to keep the world emotionally at a distance. In the beginning we share the doctor's ironical view of Catherine at her expense and feel that he is right to protect her from Morris Townsend. But in fact it can be argued that in the first half of the novel Dr Sloper (and also in some ways Mrs Penniman) regards Catherine as merely an item to be sold off in the marriage market, and an item of inferior quality not likely to bring much credit. He, Morris Townsend and Mrs Penniman, all selfishly fail to give Catherine the respect she deserves as a human being.

Nevertheless, we tend to share the doctor's ironic view of Catherine throughout the first half of the book and see her overdressing, her lack of social guile, her simplicity, the very things that make her poor material for a heroine, as comic. Later in Europe, during the scene in the Alps, Catherine and her father are far enough from all other company for the doctor to drop his ironic tone for the first time, but Catherine stubbornly refuses to give her lover up. Before she was a pathetic character; now she is stronger and is able to answer her father 'in violence' (Chapter 24). Her ability to 'stick', which before merely amused the doctor, and us, now causes him to become angry with her. He is frustrated because he cannot imagine Catherine acting from motives which he does not understand. But our perspective of Catherine has changed during the visit to Europe, from the doctor's comic ironic one of an unsuitable heroine to a new view of increased sympathy for Catherine and a harsher judgment of Dr Sloper.

The doctor's fate is itself ironic, insofar as just as the potentialities of his daughter are beginning to show themselves he can neither believe in them nor enjoy them. Catherine becomes for us a more sympathetic figure through the remainder of the novel while Dr Sloper appears more tyrannical. We now no longer feel that his ironic attacks on her are anything but sarcastic and cruel. Although the doctor does not know that Townsend has just jilted her, he knows that Catherine is suffering, so that it is cruel of him to tip his hat to her at the window (Chapter 30) in a mocking fashion that makes fun of her real agony. By the end of the novel, unable to accept that he does not know how Catherine feels, Dr Sloper becomes increasingly like Mrs Penniman. He creates roles for Catherine that Catherine herself is incapable of playing, such as his conviction that Catherine and Morris Townsend are conspiring to marry on his death. This completely unfounded belief that Catherine will marry on his death causes him to alter his will and disinherit her. He dies, unreconciled to his daughter, full of doubts that he himself has created.

Ultimately, then, Dr Sloper is a victim as much as a victimiser because of his emotional detachment and his extreme use of irony. The tables are turned on him in his conversation with Morris Townsend. Questioned by the doctor about his lack of employment Townsend finally asks ironically 'Were you kindly intending to propose something to my advantage?' (Chapter 9), thus forcing Dr Sloper to back down. The doctor condemns his daughter's actions in advance and can judge people only according to their surface appearances so that in the end, for all his intelligence, he makes mistakes. Dr Sloper's vision grows narrower as the novel goes on, and his mistakes multiply, until eventually we lose all sympathy for him.

Morris Townsend

Morris Townsend, as his name suggests, is both socially and financially an outsider who wishes to break into fashionable New York society and move 'uptown' to the best areas, such as Washington Square. He frequently exploits Mrs Penniman's ignorance of correct social behaviour to do this. Catherine says of him that 'he's more like a foreigner' (Chapter 4). Morris Townsend comes from 'town's end', the unfashionable part of town. He had been wild in his youth, speedily squandering his own small inheritance, and now lives upon the charity of his sister, Mrs Montgomery. He appears to repay her kindness by tutoring her children in Spanish but in fact he is merely using her, and Mrs Montgomery is aware of this. Morris Townsend is a person of considerable talent, good looks, force of personality and intelligence, but he is also lazy and a spendthrift. Although we are not certain of it when he first appears, it becomes increasingly obvious that Dr Sloper is correct in assuming him to be after his daughter's money. The doctor disapproves of Morris Townsend, although they are in many ways alike. The doctor admires Townsend's intelligence but says 'he is not what I call a gentleman' (Chapter 7). They are both inclined to form theories and cling to them. We are told the doctor 'rarely altered his theories' (Chapter 32) and that Townsend squandered his fortune through 'a system, a theory he had' (Chapter 6). Dr Sloper is himself a man who married advantageously, just as Morris Townsend wishes to do, and they both wish to manipulate Catherine for essentially selfish motives. They are so alike that when the doctor and Catherine are away in Europe Townsend makes himself at home in Dr Sloper's study, smoking his cigars.

Morris Townsend is essentially false, an actor. The first time Catherine meets him she feels he has 'features like young men in pictures' (Chapter 4) or 'like a statue' (Chapter 4). He talks 'the way a young man might talk in a novel' (Chapter 4). He keeps up a constant pretence of loving Catherine until near the end of the book when it becomes obvious to him that he will never gain possession of her fortune. Even then it is on the false excuse of not wanting to deprive her of her inheritance that he leaves her. He claims he is leaving her to further his business interests when it is unlikely that he is employed at all. At last we are told that 'it seemed to her that a mask had suddenly fallen from his face' (Chapter 30) and Catherine comes to see him as the liar that he really is. The one person with whom he is his real, calculating self is Mrs Penniman, in Chapter 21. He does not pretend with her in this chapter because it is not necessary; Mrs Penniman is at this point at her most self-deluded.

When his affair with Catherine is over Townsend leaves New York, travelling still, not bothering to find employment. He contracts a 'marriage of reason' for money (Chapter 34), which he had been hoping for with Catherine, and his wife dies soon afterwards. After twenty years he returns to see Catherine, partly to try to justify his past actions and partly to declare his intentions to her once more. But Catherine can see through him now and 'if she had first seen him this way she would not have liked him' (Chapter 35). Rejected, Morris Townsend departs cursing; his last word is 'Damnation!' (Chapter 35).

Mrs Penniman

We are told that Lavinia Penniman, one of the doctor's two sisters, made a foolish marriage to 'a poor clergyman, of a sickly constitution and a flowery style of eloquence, and then at the age of thirty-three had been left a widow—without children, without fortune—with nothing but the memory of Mr Penniman's flowers of speech, a certain vague aroma of which hovered about her own conversation' (Chapter 2). She comes to live in Washington Square when Catherine is ten and contrives to stay on permanently as a companion for Catherine. Mrs Penniman is in fact a rather foolish woman, disliked by Dr Sloper, with an over-active imagination. 'She was romantic; she was sentimental; she had a passion for little secrets and mysteries' (Chapter 2). This passion is so marked that Dr Sloper is able to guess that one day she will try to persuade Catherine 'that some young man with a moustache is in love with her' (Chapter 2). He rather ironically asks Mrs Penniman to make his daughter a clever woman, because he knows that Catherine is not clever and that in any case Mrs Penniman herself is too stupid to train the child's mind. She is often the target of both the doctor's and the author's irony, and James frequently uses her for comic relief.

Mrs Penniman's appearance in the novel is mainly restricted to Catherine's love affair with Morris Townsend. At first it is she who is approached by Townsend. He uses her as an excuse to get close to Catherine while still observing the proper nineteenth-century rules of behaviour. Mrs Penniman, however, rather falls for his charm and good looks and while Dr Sloper is pressing Catherine to end the relationship, Mrs Penniman persuades Catherine and Townsend to continue with it. We are told that 'she wished the plot to thicken, and the advice that she gave her niece tended, in her own imagination, to produce this result' (Chapter 15). It is she who suggests a secret marriage or an elopement because she is selfishly in love with the idea of being the romantic go-between. When the lovers are apart she exaggerates Morris Townsend's devotion to Catherine, even lies about it, and fabricates Catherine's unhappiness to Townsend, to keep the relationship alive. Later, for selfish reasons, she advises Townsend not to marry Catherine and lose Dr Sloper's inheritance, but rather to wait and see if the doctor changes his mind: Dr Sloper has threatened to turn her out of Washington Square if Catherine marries Townsend. Her name, 'Penniman', suggests the lack of pennies that forces her to live with her brother. Thus Mrs Penniman's own fears and fantasies affect Catherine's relationship with Townsend and ultimately her life, by first pushing her into an unsuitable attachment and then by delaying the marriage.

Mrs Penniman, however, manages to make things even worse. When Catherine returns from Europe, resolved to marry Morris Townsend, she finds that her aunt has been entertaining him in Washington Square for the past year. Mrs Penniman is now totally seduced by Townsend's charm and says to Catherine 'I suppose you think you know him; but you don't, my dear. You will some day, but it will only be after you have lived with him. I may almost say *I* have lived with him' (Chapter 25). Mrs Penniman now acts in Townsend's interests, not Catherine's, and advises him not to marry, as Catherine will certainly lose the inheritance money and leave him with only moderate financial means. 'She was to do her duty, quite irrespective of Catherine' (Chapter 28). In this way she destroys the relationship, because she feels it is not good enough for Morris Townsend, and in doing so she breaks Catherine's heart.

Mrs Penniman continues to live with Catherine after the affair is over, never regarded by Catherine with the same affection as she had been in the past. She disobeys Catherine by letting Townsend come to the house in the final chapter of the book and so causes Catherine the pain of seeing him in his true colours and of refusing him.

Mrs Almond

Elizabeth Almond is Dr Sloper's favourite sister, a clever woman with many children at whose house Catherine and Morris Townsend first meet. She lives some distance away in a still developing part of town which will one day become very fashionable. There she enjoys a semi-pastoral existence half in the country. She combines a cleverness, which the doctor respects, with a great deal of love and warmth so that her judgments of people and situations in *Washington Square* are usually accurate. James uses her occasionally to maintain a balance of opinions in the novel during her conversations with Dr Sloper. She tells him 'Catherine has a style of her own' and explains Catherine's lack of suitors by her seeming to all the young men to be older than themselves (Chapter 6). When Dr Sloper likens himself to a geometrical proposition because he is not so superficial as to change his mind about Townsend she says 'Doesn't geometry treat of surfaces?' (Chapter 21) and 'You are shockingly cold-blooded!' (Chapter 21). In this way she rounds out our view of the doctor's position. She is the only person in the novel who consistently cares for Catherine's welfare. Long after Catherine's resistance has turned her relationship with her father into a battle Mrs Almond can say 'If she [Catherine] is to have a fall . . . we must spread as many carpets as we can' (Chapter 27).

The background of *Washington Square*

Washington Square and *Eugénie Grandet*

Eugénie Grandet is a novel written by the French author Honoré de Balzac (1799–1850) in 1833. It is clear that James learned a lot from Balzac and in some ways used the story of Eugénie Grandet as a model for *Washington Square*. The heroine of Balzac's novel is a young woman, Eugénie, who lives with her miserly father and her mother in a French provincial town. They are visited by her cousin Charles, a spendthrift young man from Paris, who is left penniless when his father commits suicide. Charles travels to seek his fortune, but not before he and Eugénie have fallen deeply in love and Eugénie has given him a store of gold pieces given to her by her father. Eugénie's father is so furious with her for giving away her money that her mother, in distress at his rage, falls ill and dies. Eugénie waits patiently for her lover, enduring her father's anger until he too dies. At last she learns that Charles returned to Paris some time ago, a rich man once again, and has not come to see her or marry her. Eugénie gives up her inherited money and lives out her life very simply, never marrying and devoting herself to charity.

Both the characters of Catherine and Eugénie and the stories of their unhappy love affairs are very similar. But Catherine in love is different from Eugénie. Eugénie is swept away by her passion, gives Charles money and is happy to defy her father, whereas Catherine is more passive and shattered more by the difficulty of keeping her lover and yet remaining a good daughter than by simply being jilted. James's novel is not a copy.

James did borrow from Balzac, however, in his technique of putting the novel together. Like Balzac he did not limit his viewpoint to one character but moved through the minds of several. Like Balzac he opens his novel with an account of the setting and the past history of the Slopers, giving us all the information necessary for understanding the relationship between Dr Sloper and Catherine, before the main story begins. In this way when the action begins the story moves easily. Again like Balzac, James gives a brief resumé of subsequent events at the end of *Washington Square* so that the story is enfolded neatly between the beginning and the end. Lastly James noticed the ability with which Balzac economically sketched in his settings and his quick, telling analyses of how environment affects character. James did the same with the same effectiveness in such passages as 'In a country in which, to play a social part, you must either earn your income or make believe that you earn it, the healing art has appeared in a high degree to combine two recognised sources of credit' (Chapter 1).

James managed to improve upon Balzac's techniques, however, by entering all his characters' minds but focusing attention principally upon Catherine. All the actions and opinions of others in the book matter only insofar as they relate to Catherine and this unity and economy are unique to James. *Eugénie Grandet* frequently lets its interest wander to old Mr Grandet and his money matters while *Washington Square* is a much more compact work of a novelist's craft.

Imagery

Not surprisingly in a novel which deals with the victimisation of the heroine, there is a great deal of imagery of knives and killing in the book. After she has been jilted Catherine writes to Morris Townsend 'Dear Morris, you are killing me!' (Chapter 30) and her father says of her European trip 'we have fattened the sheep for him before he [Townsend] kills it' (Chapter 24). Mrs Penniman asks Dr Sloper 'Don't you wish also by chance to murder your child?' (Chapter 19) and tells him later 'I will answer you with your own weapons' (Chapter 27). She is described in the following way: 'If Morris had been her son, she would have certainly sacrificed Catherine to a superior conception of his future.... Nevertheless, it checked her breath a little to have the sacrificial knife, as it were, suddenly thrust into her hand' (Chapter 28). James uses these images with all the major characters in *Washington Square* to show that they are all guilty of ill-treating Catherine.

Another telling image that runs throughout *Washington Square* is that of houses. Dr Sloper's house in Washington Square is described in this way: 'This structure, and many of its neighbours, which it exactly resembled, were supposed, forty years ago, to embody the last results of architectural science, and they remain to this day very solid and honourable dwellings' (Chapter 3). Although the doctor may not always be 'solid and honourable' in his dealings with his daughter this is how he would like to see himself and his position in New York society. Most of the scenes in the novel take place inside the Sloper house in Washington Square, and this helps to give a sense of Catherine's isolation from the outside world. It is within this house that Catherine, throughout the book, is largely confined, and from it the novel takes its name. It is fear of being cast out from Washington Square that causes Mrs Penniman to advise Morris Townsend to delay marrying Catherine in secret, so ruining the relationship.

From Mrs Almond's house in a semi-pastoral environment we can guess at the inner goodness of her nature. From Mrs Montgomery's 'magnified baby-house' (Chapter 14) Dr Sloper is able to deduce that its owner is 'a thrifty and self-respecting little person—the modest proportions of her dwelling seemed to indicate that she was of small stature—who took a virtuous satisfaction in keeping herself tidy, and had resolved that, since she might not be splendid, she would at least be immaculate' (Chapter 14). From the homeless Morris Townsend's view of the doctor's residence we learn a lot about Townsend's character. Refused by Dr Sloper as a suitor, Townsend sees the door of the house as 'the closed portal of happiness' (Chapter 16), and from his thinking it 'a devilish comfortable house' (Chapter 16) we realise that Washington Square symbolises a social position which he would like to acquire. Townsend's moment of greatest triumph comes when he can sit in the doctor's study, in the heart of the house, while Dr Sloper and his daughter are away in Europe.

James and melodrama

Washington Square could easily have been a very melodramatic story, since it is really just a variation on the classic fairy tale of cruel father (Dr Sloper), motherless daughter (Catherine), handsome lover (Morris Townsend) and fairy godmother (Mrs Penniman). If James had written his story less carefully it would have been very sentimental, using stereotypes instead of characters who seem like real people. The comedy in the story prevents the plot from becoming too serious and makes the story seem new.

First of all, James's ironic tone prevents us from taking the characters too seriously. He makes fun of his heroine, Catherine, in the first half of the novel, of Dr Sloper in the second half, and of Mrs Penniman

The role of emotion in *Washington Square*

Thought and feeling

The characters in *Washington Square* all have one feature in their
personalities which dominates their outlook. Dr Sloper is dominated
by his intellect and believes 'You are good for nothing unless you are
clever' (Chapter 2). His cleverness has enabled him to marry well, build
up a reputable medical practice and, he feels, become an expert judge
of his daughter's suitors. This dominance of his intellect continues
throughout the novel until the very moment of his death, which he cor-
rectly diagnoses. Morris Townsend likewise has a keen intellect which
he uses to deceive Catherine in his ruthless pursuit of wealth and status.
He sees Catherine as a means of gaining control of the house at

Washington Square. He is prepared to manipulate Mrs Penniman and live on his sister's charity in order to gain a position that, he thinks, he is by nature suited to enjoy because of his superior intellect.

Mrs Penniman, on the other hand, is dominated by an excess of sentimental and romantic feeling which drives out all common sense. Her thoughts and actions are foolish. 'She would have liked to have a lover, and to correspond with him under an assumed name, in letters left at a shop' (Chapter 2). At the close of the book this same sentimentality causes her to allow Morris Townsend to see Catherine once again, although Catherine's passions are long dead. Catherine too, at the beginning of the novel, is so oppressed by her awareness of her father's disappointment at her intellectual dullness that she is capable of nothing except passive feelings obedient to her father's will. Only Mrs Almond and, to a lesser extent, Mrs Montgomery combine mental perceptiveness with compassion, and they are on the periphery of the book. *Washington Square* would be a very different novel if Mrs Almond instead of Mrs Penniman were Catherine's mentor.

Whereas the qualities of the other characters remain fixed throughout the book, Catherine, and Catherine alone, develops and changes from a character dominated by feeling to one guided by intellect. She has been brought up to believe in her own mental dullness and to idolise her clever father. Because she lacks vivacity and brilliance her intelligence has no chance to attract notice. Instead she has only very simple feelings of duty, truthfulness and integrity. Her sense of dress is extravagantly opulent because it is never tempered by what Dr Sloper calls 'the beauty of *reason*' (Chapter 2). The narrator of the novel, along with Dr Sloper, reminds us constantly of Catherine's intellectual mediocrity, emphasising instead her good health and robustness. When she meets Morris Townsend and is completely taken in by his superficial beauty and charming manner the narrator's judgment seems to be confirmed.

Under the pressure of her affair with Townsend, however, Catherine slowly gains in power of intellect and observation. The first person she begins to see through is her aunt who, Catherine comes to realise, is a selfish, scheming person. Everyone else has understood Mrs Penniman long ago. As Dr Sloper tries to force Catherine to give up her suitor—a process culminating in the threatening scene in the Swiss mountains— she begins to see her father less as a god and more as a human being. She begins to find faults in him, and this leads up to her accusation that he is treating her badly. This is succeeded by her realisation that 'the great facts of her career were that Morris Townsend had trifled with her affection, and that her father had broken its spring' (Chapter 32). In the course of the book Catherine comes to a more balanced, intellectualised view of her father than the awe and obedience she previously felt—so much so that she will even refuse his dying wish that she should promise not to marry Morris Townsend. This is not because she wants to marry him but because she thinks the request unfair.

Catherine's perceptiveness undergoes a final test when Morris Townsend returns to court her again at the close of the book. Her judgment of him is dispassionate and devastating. 'If she had first seen him this way she would not have liked him' (Chapter 35) and 'Morris was embarrassed, but Catherine gave him no help' (Chapter 35). By the end of *Washington Square* she has grown to be intelligent and perceptive, but this knowledge comes too late to help her.

Whereas Catherine's intellect is balanced by an ability to feel, Dr Sloper is completely dominated by his intellect. He takes great pride in his ability as a physician and although nobody blames him for the death of his wife and son he blames himself so that 'he walked under the weight of this very private censure for the rest of his days, and bore forever the scars of a castigation to which the strongest hand he knew had treated him on the night that followed his wife's death' (Chapter 1). He suffers from imposing his own intellectual standard on everyone else, a standard which not even he can measure up to. The result is his cruelty, his ironical attitude to his daughter and his overconfidence in his ability to judge character.

When Dr Sloper grows so concerned with his own cleverness that being proved right is his sole object he is capable of becoming quite inhuman. For him, measuring his mind against his daughter is only a game. 'This idea of Catherine "sticking" appeared to have a comical side, and to offer a prospect of entertainment' (Chapter 18). When Catherine refuses steadfastly to give up her lover he is surprised. When she suggests that she should not continue to live in his house, since she is going to marry against his wishes, the doctor is sure that this idea is Morris Townsend's. It seems too clever for Catherine. He hopes to isolate Catherine by taking her to Europe but there she becomes utterly steadfast in her opposition to his wishes. The doctor grows angry, and in a moment of self-revelation exclaims 'I am not a very good man. Though I am very smooth externally, at bottom I am very passionate; and I assure you, I can be very hard' (Chapter 24). After this he threatens to abandon her in the Alps. When he is unable to get his way, the passion that lies at the base of his nature becomes violent.

Yet it is this passion in the depths of his nature which prevents Dr Sloper, despite his unyielding character, from seeming merely one-dimensional. He is a man of strong feeling who has subordinated this side of his nature to his intellect. Morris Townsend is also a man who has subordinated his feelings to his powers of rational calculation. Essentially he is in love with himself and his own abilities and sees in marrying a rich woman a way of raising himself to his true status. He suppresses his distaste in making advances to an unattractive woman, and although, like everyone else, he finds Catherine dull, he showers her with affection. He dislikes Mrs Penniman nearly as much as the doctor does yet he goes through a show of admiration and attentiveness with her.

In many ways Morris Townsend is the counterpart of the doctor. Like Dr Sloper he has an excellent mind and is often inclined to see people as little more than instruments to be used. He lives on his sister and manipulates Mrs Penniman and Catherine. He cleverly exploits his charm, good looks and intellect to deceive them all. He and the doctor have a sort of grudging admiration for each other.

The reason why Townsend delays marrying Catherine in the hope of gaining her father's consent is that in doing so he hopes to lay his hands on a further twenty thousand dollars. His actions then are governed by the logic of economics and his own estimation of his worth. Seventeen years later, when he visits Catherine again, he does this because he has grown older and knows that his market value has declined. He will accept her now on her reduced inheritance. Economics, rather than the fact that Townsend does not love her, is also the chief reason for Dr Sloper's disapproval of the match. He feels that Townsend is fortune-hunting and is unsuitable because he has no money and is unlikely to find respectable employment.

Catherine is the heroine of *Washington Square* and the only character in the novel to move from an either emotionally or intellectually dominated viewpoint to a balanced one. But James is careful not to glamorise or sentimentalise this change. Catherine's awakened perceptiveness is not accompanied by any change in manner. She still lacks vivacity, wit or charm, even though she is now quite capable of reviewing her own situation accurately. 'Nothing could ever undo the wrong or cure the pain that Morris had inflicted on her, and nothing could ever make her feel towards her father as she felt in her younger years. There was something dead in her life, and her duty was to try and fill the void' (Chapter 32). Too much damage has been done to her and she can neither love nor marry the two very eligible suitors who later court her with Dr Sloper's approval.

Despite these changes in her character, Catherine's outward manner after being jilted by Morris Townsend seems remarkably similar to her behaviour before his appearance. To this extent *Washington Square* is very much a novel about misleading appearances. Dr Sloper, a calmly detached man of the world, is in fact driven by intellectual self-obsession. Morris Townsend only *appears* a gentleman. Mrs Penniman, supposedly devoted to promoting Catherine's romantic interests, is more interested in her own vicarious pleasure and secretly wishes to take Catherine's place. Catherine, presented to us as 'the softest creature in the world' (Chapter 2), grows to become the novel's stead-fast heroine.

Psychology in *Washington Square*

Psychology is crucial in *Washington Square*. Since the psychological probing of characters is a hallmark of the modern novel, this is no doubt one of the reasons why *Washington Square* still seems modern when other novels of the late nineteenth century seem out of date. Henry James's elder brother, William, was an eminent psychologist and James himself always took a great interest in the psychology of his characters. With Catherine he has created a heroine who is extremely naive and during the novel comes slowly and painfully to a knowledge of herself and others. The other two central characters, Dr Sloper and Morris Townsend, understand themselves and one another very well, but despite their self-interest they both fail to gain their ends.

In many ways the plot of *Washington Square* concerns the very old story of the weak triumphing over the strong. Throughout the book Catherine appears weak or helpless by reason of her naivety, her timid-ity and her sense of duty. Yet in the long run she frustrates two very clever men, her father and her suitor, and comes to realise that they have treated her badly. It is the psychology of the characters as James portrays them that prevents *Washington Square* from seeming exces-sively simple or dominated by clichés. Because psychology, rather than plot, is central to the book, the story moves forward not through author-manipulated actions or events, but rather through the motives and interactions of complexly conceived characters. Thus the story of Dr Sloper's and Townsend's intrigues, of Catherine's gradual matur-ing and awakening from illusion, is made to seem inevitable. James has his characters appear to work out their own destinies.

The story begins with a description of Dr Sloper. He is a clever, successful and proud man, bringing up his daughter with 'a stock of unexpended authority, by which the child, in its early years, profited largely' (Chapter 1). James mentions the guilt the doctor feels for the deaths of his wife and son, which must affect his relationship with his daughter, but James is careful to make Dr Sloper seem neither a mon-ster responsible for the deaths nor an object of pity because of them. The author's tone is light. 'For a man whose trade was to keep people alive he had certainly done poorly in his own family' (Chapter 1). The result is that Dr Sloper sees his daughter as someone who ought to be worthy of his price but who unfortunately is not clever enough to achieve this. These two opposing images in the doctor's mind, of Catherine's potential and the reality of her nature, govern his attitude towards her. This leads to the inconsistency of his asking Mrs Penniman to 'Try and make a clever woman of her, Lavinia' (Chapter 2) and his ironical attitude to his daughter. This leads him to 'a certain oddity of reasoning. "I expect nothing," he said to himself; "so that, if she gives me a surprise, it will be all clear gain. If she doesn't, it will be no loss." ' (Chapter 2). This is the sort of self-deception which leads Dr Sloper to take pride in not interfering with Catherine's love affair, while at the same time putting as much pressure on her as possible so as to influence her decision.

Catherine is presented to us next after Dr Sloper in the novel. James wants to portray her as an ordinary, undistinguished person while at the same time leaving enough margin for her to develop extraordinary qualities later on. Thus he presents her intellectual mediocrity to us from her father's point of view, to make it seem less than it might be in reality, and makes frequent mention of her physical good health and robustness. Catherine is not shown as having any charm, quickness of wit or vivacity, but we are told that she is 'much addicted to telling the truth' (Chapter 2), that 'she was extremely fond of her father, and very much afraid of him' (Chapter 2) and 'Her deepest desire was to please him' (Chapter 2). This hints at an extraordinary integrity that surfaces later in *Washington Square* and governs many of Catherine's actions.

At first Catherine seems very malleable because there is no conflict between 'her deepest desire [to please her father]' and any other wish. Catherine is innocent of self-pity, resentment, vanity or spite, and, unlike her father, she is without any feeling of pride with which to make claims: 'Love demands certain things as a right; but Catherine had no sense of her rights; she had only a consciousness of immense and unexpected favours' (Chapter 8). Since she herself feels neither suppressed envy nor antipathy she is incapable of sensing such emotions in others. She never once feels suspicious of the motives of a suitor like Morris Townsend, never once asks herself why he may be interested in her. Analysis is more in her father's way of thinking. Yet this absolute innocence is in itself rather extraordinary.

When in Chapter 10 Morris Townsend visits Washington Square to declare his love for Catherine he initiates a game between himself, Dr Sloper and Catherine which will continue throughout the book. 'We must settle something—we must take a line' (Chapter 10) Townsend declares, staring at himself in the doctor's mirror, full of self-love rather than love for Catherine. His attention is next drawn to 'a back-gammon-board folded together in the shape of two volumes' (Chapter 10) at the base of the mirror, then to thoughts of Dr Sloper. 'If Morris had been pleased to describe the master of the house as a heartless scoffer, it is because he thought him too much on his guard, and this was the easiest way to express his own dissatisfaction—a dissatisfaction which he had made a point of concealing from the Doctor'

(Chapter 10). In this way the idea of a game having begun is made explicit.

The game is set in motion by Morris Townsend as a way of engaging Dr Sloper in battle, but it involves Catherine, and she plays by different rules from those of the two men in her life. This inconsistency engenders much of the story's action. Dr Sloper and Morris Townsend are engaged in a ruthless, unsentimental struggle for power, one in which they are fully prepared to sacrifice Catherine's feelings, while she responds to them only with the logic of love. When both her father's and her lover's moves are blocked—the doctor's by her refusal to give up her lover, Townsend's by her refusal to marry against her father's wishes—then their pride is hurt and they become resentful. When Catherine feels that they both despise her love she quietly but completely withdraws it from them. In this way they, who were at first invulnerable, are finally made dependent upon her. Catherine, who was at first so vulnerable, becomes in the end independent. Mrs Penniman is also a schemer, involved in the power game, but she acts in a less obvious, and, above all, sentimental way. Her egoistic pride is romantic. She derives her happiness from arranging an elopement or, later, a reconciliation attempt. She understands the men in her way but she cannot understand Catherine. Later in the novel Catherine realises what Mrs Penniman has done and reproaches her aunt for meddling, whereupon Mrs Penniman takes refuge in self-pity.

Catherine's advancement as a character in *Washington Square* towards a position of self-awareness is a growth from a passivity lacking any will of her own to a rooted firmness. She is first presented to us in the novel as shy, unassuming, inarticulate and adoring. She meets Morris Townsend at Mrs Almond's party and, completely without suspicion, falls in love with this handsome, self-assured and fair-spoken man. But it is at this point that we are given the first hint of her potential will. Catherine dissembles for the first time in her life. She tells Marian Almond that she thinks 'nothing particular' (Chapter 4) of Morris Townsend. Later to her father and aunt Penniman she says 'I am rather tired' (Chapter 4) when 'Catherine was not so easily tired as all that'. Her third lie comes when she denies knowing Townsend's name, and James goes on to add 'with all his irony, her father believed her' (Chapter 4).

The next step in the growth of Catherine's will is marked by her response after Townsend's second visit to Washington Square to her father's insensitive question 'Well, my dear, did he propose to you today?' (Chapter 6)—to which she replies 'Perhaps he will do it next time' (Chapter 6). This comes after Dr Sloper has just confirmed to himself 'Decidedly . . . my daughter is not brilliant' and the effect is that 'The Doctor stood staring; he wondered whether his daughter were serious'. Catherine even imagines herself answering more boldly 'Oh yes, Mr Morris Townsend proposed to me, and I refused him'. All this hints at the potential will that begins to take shape after her father openly opposes Morris Townsend as a suitor. When he and Townsend come into open conflict and it becomes necessary for Catherine to make a decision, then her will slowly begins to form. She does not follow her aunt Penniman's advice to appeal for her father's pity, and at the same time she has no intention of giving up her lover. Instead she begins to wonder how she can move her father to give his consent.

Later, during her one-year travels with Dr Sloper across Europe Catherine comes to realise that her father's opposition is not motivated by love and that he secretly dislikes her. She cuts herself off from him entirely and says to her aunt on her return in an unusually firm tone 'I shall never plead with [my father] for anything; that is all over. He has put me off. I am come home to be married' (Chapter 25). To Morris Townsend she declares with the same new firmness 'It is a great thing to be separated from your father, when you have worshipped him before. It has made me very unhappy; or it would have made me so if I didn't love you' and she goes on 'I will never ask him for anything again, or expect anything from him' (Chapter 26). How terrible therefore it is for her to find that Morris Townsend loves her no more than her father does. It leaves her at last reluctantly independent and totally without support.

Thus the plot of *Washington Square* shows Catherine being deeply hurt by both her father and Morris Townsend during her growth to maturity. The close of the novel shows the revenge which she takes upon them. Throughout the book Morris Townsend's goal is constant. He aims to get the inheritance from Catherine's father as well as the money she already has from her mother and he is confused by Catherine's changes of heart. Catherine's goal in the book is also constant, to marry Morris Townsend, with her father's consent if possible but without it if necessary. She is confused by Townsend's changes in strategy. When Townsend hears that the doctor has returned from Europe without changing his mind he continues the game theme by saying 'I don't like to be beaten' (Chapter 26). Catherine, although not understanding the nature of the conflict, responds with the same self-assured directness that characterises her on her return from abroad: 'How are you beaten if we marry?' Townsend has been caught between a fear of losing the father's money through elopement if he fails at length to convince Dr Sloper of his sincerity, and a fear of losing everything if he delays too long. He is now forced to break off. It is precisely the dead issue of coming between father and daughter which he uses as an excuse, and Catherine comes to realise that she has been deceived.

Catherine's grief is great, partly because she is too proud to share it with her aunt, and, grieving, she breaks with Morris Townsend as she did before with her father. 'It seemed to her that she had given Morris up' (Chapter 30). Thus she is sufficiently detached from the memory of her love for him to remain calm when years later he appears again. Dr Sloper was wrong in predicting a life of pleasure for him; after years of failure Morris Townsend returns and gives in to Mrs Penniman's sentimental idea that he still has influence over Catherine's heart. When they meet Catherine responds to his conversation with a series of negatives 'I think we had better not.... I don't think you ought to have come.... I did not understand.... I don't think it is necessary' (Chapter 35). Then she goes on calmly to inform him that she feels no resentment, but that she will not allow any affection for him to re-enter her heart. 'I can't begin again—I can't take it up. Everything is dead and buried. It was too serious; it made a great change in my life' (Chapter 35). Her 'little dry manner' (Chapter 35) forces Morris Townsend into ignominious retreat.

Catherine also takes her revenge on her father. Dr Sloper begins by taking a rather cruel pleasure in watching his daughter while she suffers what he knows to be an agonising conflict of loyalties. When she no longer seems to be suffering he no longer appears to be curious. Dr Sloper is puzzled, rather than pleased, to hear that she has broken off the engagement. He says nastily 'You are rather cruel, after encouraging him and playing with him for so long!' and James comments 'The Doctor had his revenge, after all' (Chapter 31), but it seems to be a revenge directed against Catherine's new independence rather than towards gaining what Dr Sloper wanted, the withdrawal of Morris Townsend.

Still suspicious, Dr Sloper tells his daughter that he will cut her out of his will unless she promises not to marry Morris Townsend after his death. Catherine had offered to do this before she distanced herself from her father (Chapter 18) but now she replies not that she won't but that she can't make such a promise, thus causing the doctor to believe that she will indeed marry after his death. He alters his will, knowing that the additional money means nothing to Catherine, then lives out his remaining days miserably convinced that despite his new will the couple will marry as soon as he is dead. Catherine, for her part, does nothing to assuage such fears and Dr Sloper dies before the final scene, in which Catherine rejects Townsend, has taken place.

Thus the novel's heroine, Catherine, takes revenge of sorts on those who had injured her. If we take this view of *Washington Square* the final chapters will be seen very much as a demonstration of Catherine's pride. We do not know whether James himself was aware of it (the effect would have been too remarkable for him to let it pass without making some comment upon it) but by the close of the novel Catherine is very much her father's daughter. Catherine's pride, by the end of *Washington Square*, is parallel to that of Dr Sloper and Morris Townsend. She has become as inflexible and uncompromising as they are, and although, unlike them, she can love, she does not possess Mrs Almond's sympathetic ability to share warmly another person's point of view. In his next book, *The Portrait of a Lady*, James was to call this 'the imagination of loving'.

James writes that Catherine 'was conscious of no aptitude for organised resentment' (Chapter 30) but the way she distances herself emotionally from both her suitor and her father so completely suggests an unconscious desire for revenge. Catherine might have been a dumbly loyal wife to Morris Townsend if she had not been forced to give him up. By the end of the novel she has buried the emotional side of her nature and will not allow it to be revived. When Morris Townsend comes to see Catherine again he says it is because

'for many years it has been the desire of my life that we should be friends again.'
'That is impossible.'
'Why so? Not if you will allow it.'
'I will not allow it,' said Catherine. (Chapter 35)

In her proud isolation Catherine has come very close to Dr Sloper's original intellectual position of 'I expect nothing' (Chapter 2).

Psychology then is crucial to the way James has conceived *Washington Square* and put the novel together. What interested him in the story Mrs Kemble told which provided the inspiration for the novel was not the possibilities of the plot which were all clichés, but the psychology of a young woman placed in such a position as Catherine. It is psychological interaction, rather than twists in a complex plot, that moves the story along, in this case to a most remarkable conclusion.

Part 4

Hints for study

There can be no better preparation for an examination in literature than to read the novel you have been studying at least twice. So after you have read *Washington Square* and these Notes read Henry James's novel again. This will allow you to feel comfortable with the book, and a re-reading of the novel with these Notes in mind will help you to see far more clearly how James put *Washington Square* together. You will find that it will also help you to recall details which will be useful as examples with which to back up your arguments in examination answers. In examinations it is not always necessary to be able to quote accurately from the text (although a number of useful quotations are supplied later); examiners do not expect candidates to have super-human memories. It will be necessary, however, for you to justify any arguments you put forward by referring to the events of the novel. If you write about Henry James's theme of visiting Europe as a way of growing to maturity you should then mention that Catherine, for example, visits Europe for a year and returns with the self-assurance and maturity to defy her father openly. It is not necessary to quote from the text that Mrs Penniman 'observing [Catherine] set it down to foreign travel, which had made her more positive, more mature'. But a second reading of the text will allow you to back up all your arguments with general references to the book.

When writing your answer it is best to use a formal style of writing (such as has been used in these Notes). Notice that it is best always to refer to events in the novel in the present tense, for example, 'in the middle of the book Dr Sloper visits Mrs Montgomery and learns from her that Morris Townsend is a spendthrift, too lazy to work, and mercenary. She begs Dr Sloper not to let Townsend marry Catherine'. Likewise it is common to refer to the author's use of various techniques in the present tense— 'James uses irony and comedy to prevent his characters from becoming too much like the fairy tale types which they resemble'.

Preparing your answers

When you have decided which literature question you are going to answer in your examination paper the first thing you should do is not begin to write but consider what you are going to write. Try to think about the question topic and note down in brief phrases any points that occur to you which might be useful in your answer. Note them down either on a piece of spare paper or in your answer booklet (cross them out later; examiners must ignore anything in your booklet you have crossed out, and in fact will approve of evidence that you have obviously planned your answer). Noting down some brief points will serve to remind you what to write later on and will actually help to stimulate your mind to come up with new points. It is worthwhile spending quite a lot of time on this simple contemplation of points on which to base your answer. If you plan to spend forty-five minutes on your entire answer you should spend about fifteen of them making notes on what you will write later, that is, about one-third of your answer time. This may seem quite a lot, but in fact when you begin to write your answer you will be able to write much more quickly, because you will be spared the burden of wondering what to write next and in what order to write down your ideas.

When you have listed your points, look at them and write down a number beside each one to indicate the order in which you want to present them. Some will obviously go together. In a question asking you to 'Discuss ... ', for example, you will be presenting both sides of the issue. Your answer will consist either of a series of contrasting pairs of arguments, or of one line of argument contradicted halfway through by a stronger, contrasting line. You are now in a position to see the line of your argument and can arrange your points in a logical sequence. This ordering will allow you to see the overall shape of your essay, what arguments will follow well one after another and where it is a good idea to break off and introduce an entirely new argument. Once you know the order and shape of your answer, you will have a rough idea where the halfway mark in it is likely to be. Therefore if you have, for example, half an hour remaining, you should reach that halfway mark roughly after fifteen minutes. If after the first fifteen minutes you find that you are behind schedule you will know that you have to speed up, write faster, mention your points more quickly and with fewer examples. If you find yourself ahead of schedule you will know that you ought to slow down, spend more time on details and put in more examples from the text.

If you have several answers to write in your examination, spend no more time on each answer than you have allowed for, even if you cannot finish the answer. In an examination the first fifty per cent of the marks awarded for an answer are the easiest to get. But if you are aiming for higher than average marks, your answers will have to be very much better than average to gain these extra marks. Bearing this in mind you will find it more profitable to spread your time evenly over your answers than to spend almost all your time on one question and only briefly touch on the rest. For example, two medium length answers to two questions are likely to earn you twenty-five per cent each, a total of fifty per cent, and a pass. Spending all of your time answering one of the questions and only touching on the other one is likely to earn you thirty-five per cent and ten per cent, a total of forty-five per cent, or a failure.

When you begin your answer try to write it as a series of claims or arguments; for example, '*Washington Square* is a novel that makes little use of background because James felt America was an unsuitable place to write about; therefore he focuses attention on his characters and the conflicts between them and inside them . . . ' and so on. Wherever possible support each new point in your argument with an example from the text. This both proves your argument to be true and shows that you have read the book carefully. When writing about technique it is always useful to say why it is significant for the novel, that is, how the author used it to make a better book. It is no good simply listing examples of knife imagery in *Washington Square*; you must show why this imagery makes the book effective—by reminding us that all the characters are guilty of metaphorically 'killing' Catherine.

Quotations

Quotations from the text should be always made clear by being enclosed in quotation marks—'Mrs Penniman was truly amiable, but she now gave signs of temper.' Marks indicating the characters' direct speech should be enclosed within the quotation marks—'"Ah, the dear little kittens," cried Mrs Penniman.' Should you choose to leave part of the quotation out, because it is not relevant to your purposes, show the omission by introducing three dots where the missing material would have been. So 'The Doctor had time to take cognizance of these details; for Mrs Montgomery, whose conduct he pronounced under the circumstances inexcusable, kept him waiting some ten minutes before she appeared' could be shortened to 'The Doctor had time to take cognizance of these details; for Mrs Montgomery . . . kept him waiting some ten minutes before she appeared.' Should you wish to add a word to a quotation, in order to make it clear who is being referred to, introduce the word within square brackets [ ]. '"I don't know," said Catherine—"I don't know what he [Dr Sloper] thinks."'

If you are planning to memorise some quotations for use in your examination answers, try to choose ones which can be used in a variety of contexts. This reduces the chances of your work being wasted. Here are some useful quotations (you will not need to learn in which chapter they occur):

'The little girl was a disappointment' (Chapter 1), Dr Sloper's view of the young Catherine.

'In reality, she was the softest creature in the world' (Chapter 2), Catherine's character.

'He had features like young men in pictures' (Chapter 4), Catherine's view of Morris Townsend.

'He almost never addressed his daughter save in the ironical form' (Chapter 4), Dr Sloper's usual way of speaking to Catherine.

'He is not what I call a gentleman' (Chapter 7), Dr Sloper on Morris Townsend.

'I don't want to believe in you' (Chapter 12), Dr Sloper speaking to Morris Townsend.

'Don't let her marry him!' (Chapter 14), Mrs Montgomery speaking to Dr Sloper.

'The woman's an idiot!' (Chapter 16), Morris Townsend's thoughts on Mrs Penniman.

'He was sorry for her . . . but he was so sure he was right' (Chapter 18), Dr Sloper on Catherine.

'Catherine loves you so much that you may do anything' (Chapter 21), Mrs Penniman speaking to Morris Townsend.

'He is not very fond of me' (Chapter 26), Catherine's view of her father on her return from Europe.

'It seemed to her that a mask had suddenly fallen from his face' (Chapter 30), Catherine's view of Morris Townsend after she has been jilted.

'Morris Townsend had trifled with her affection and . . . her father had broken its spring' (Chapter 32), Catherine after she has been jilted.

'for life, as it were' (Chapter 35), the picture of entrapment and paralysis on which the novel closes.

Revision

The following brief notes on *Washington Square* are useful points to remember for revision purposes.

—*Washington Square* is a novel with very few background 'paraphernalia' and so the focus of the novel is on action between characters and within themselves, rather than between character and environment.

—James writes *Washington Square* in an impersonal style so that he never intrudes in his own person to make moral judgments on his characters.

—Extra information is given to us by James through his use of irony (saying one thing and meaning another). Also we share Dr Sloper's comically ironic view of Catherine through the first half of the book. We depart from this viewpoint in the second half to see Catherine less ironically and more sympathetically, and to see the doctor less sympathetically with James's irony directed more at him.

—Catherine is torn between her father, Morris Townsend and Mrs Penniman, all of whom use her selfishly for their own ends, the doctor to prove an intellectual point, Morris Townsend to marry money, and Mrs Penniman to satisfy her romantic fantasies.

—It is during her visit to Europe that Catherine finally rejects her father and returns, more mature and less pitiful, to see through Morris Townsend in the end.

—Morris Townsend is an outsider who wishes to enter rich and fashionable New York society and move 'uptown'. He is in fact very like Dr Sloper at the beginning of his career.

—James uses comedy to prevent his characters from slipping into melodramatic stereotypes. This allows the one scene that is not touched by comedy, the scene in the Alps, to appear especially dramatic.

Sample questions and answers

Discuss the importance of setting in *Washington Square*.

It has been said that setting is of no importance at all to *Washington Square* and James himself complained about the lack of background 'paraphernalia' necessary to write the novel. He believed that Europe, with its richer cultural heritage, was the proper setting for fiction. Despite this, James is able to use descriptive detail to sketch in his settings where necessary. His 'grassy waysides of Canal Street', his autobiographical descriptions of children walking round Washington Square and his ability swiftly to evoke Mrs Penniman's walk along Fifth Avenue or her visit to an oyster saloon are all very effective in giving us an idea of what these places must have been like.

But setting is of secondary importance in *Washington Square* for other reasons. Rather than being a book about a particular area in New York, *Washington Square* is essentially a novel about characters. It is concerned more with the conflicts between Dr Sloper, Catherine and Morris Townsend, and with Catherine's inner conflicts, than with their interaction with the setting. James's prime interest is in chronicling the changes that occur in Catherine's psychology, in noting how and why these changes occur. Not for nothing was the author's brother, William James, one of the most famous psychologists before Sigmund Freud (1856–1939), the Austrian founder of psychoanalysis.

It is significant, however, that it is after a change of setting, Catherine's journey to the older culture of Europe, that she becomes mature enough to see through Morris Townsend and finally conclude 'You treated me badly'. It is after her father's terrifying words in the Swiss Alps that she grows strong enough to defy him, and we feel that only in a place as isolated as the Alps could Dr Sloper have dropped 'the ironic form' to address his daughter in a straightforward fashion.

Setting may be of secondary importance, but New York, which James frequently presents as a bustling boom town, is in the end the best setting for the book. The New York of *Washington Square* is a city where people are ambitious, constantly wishing to move 'uptown', and this is the reason for Morris Townsend's attempts to marry Catherine and her money. Dr Sloper himself did the same thing years ago when he married his wealthy wife, even if he did do so for love as well.

At the same time, paralleling Townsend's attempts to move uptown by marriage, we see his symbolic progress through the main setting of the book, the house in Washington Square itself. At the start of the book he appears in the front parlour of the house where guests are usually received, ingratiates his way into the doctor's study during Dr Sloper's absence, and is eventually forced back into the parlour again, and then out of the house. We can gauge Morris Townsend's success by his progress through the novel's setting. Thus despite its relative unimportance in this novel of character, the setting is quickly and skilfully drawn by James and has its part to play.

Discuss James's use of comedy in *Washington Square*.

Traditionally comedies have happy endings, and when Morris Townsend is finally driven away and Catherine settles down to sit 'for life, as it were' we cannot feel that *Washington Square* has closed on a happy note. It is, however, comic in many other respects. Not the least of these is that it can be a very entertaining and funny book. James tells us that Dr Sloper is successful because 'there was nothing abstract in his remedies—he always ordered you to take something', and he can be equally amusing when describing his other characters. He tells us at a party that Marian Almond has 'a very small figure and a very big sash' or says Mrs Penniman 'was not absolutely veracious; but this defect was of no great consequence, for she never had anything to conceal'. Indeed his ironic attacks on Mrs Penniman in particular are often very comic, and comic relief seems to be one of her main functions in the book.

A feature of irony is that it is often comic and James uses the ironical form frequently throughout the bok. He not only writes of his characters ironically, for example saying Mrs Penniman 'reflected that her own great use in the world was owing to her aptitude for many things', but also has his characters address each other ironically. The doctor seldom speaks to Catherine in any other tone, saying to her 'Is it possible that this magnificent person is my child?' when she is plainly overdressed. These comic subtleties enrich the language of the book and make for more entertaining reading. This matters since the plot of *Washington Square* is too thin to hold the reader's attention on its own.

The plot and characters of *Washington Square* come very close to melodrama. A wicked father (Dr Sloper) tries to prevent the heroine (Catherine) from marrying the man she loves (Morris Townsend). James often uses comic devices to keep his characters from turning into fairy-tale types. Thus Catherine who is plain, physically robust, very shy and intellectually rather dull is unconventional material for a fairy-tale heroine. We see Morris Townsend, who tells Catherine that he 'liked everything to be natural', annoyed because 'he had omitted, by accident, to say that he would sing for her if she would play to him'. James frequently uses the comic Mrs Penniman to exaggerate and thus make fun of many of the novel's more melodramatic scenes. By using comedy to reduce events to a more mundane level, James prevents his characters or plot from appearing melodramatic. Comedy, therefore, allows him to write a seemingly realistic novel filled with ordinary people, in a way that is still entertaining and pleasant to read.

Part 5

Suggestions for further reading

The text

JAMES, HENRY: *Washington Square*, Penguin Books, Harmondsworth, 1963. The most easily available text, used in preparing these Notes.

Other works by James

NOVELS: *Roderick Hudson, The American, The Europeans, The Portrait of a Lady, The Bostonians, The Princess Casamassima, The Tragic Muse, The Spoils of Poynton, What Maisie Knew, The Awkward Age, The Sacred Fount, The Ambassadors, The Wings of a Dove, The Golden Bowl* (Most of these are available from Penguin Books, Harmondsworth, or The Bodley Head, London).

NON-FICTION: *The American Scene*, Rupert Hart-Davis, London, 1968.

The House of Fiction, Essays on the Novel by Henry James, ed. Leon Edel, Rupert Hart-Davis, London, 1957.

Henry James: Selected Literary Criticism, ed. Morris Shapiro, Penguin Books, Harmondsworth, 1968.

The Art of the Novel: Critical Prefaces by Henry James, ed. R.P. Blackmur, Charles Scribner's Sons, New York, 1934.

The Notebooks of Henry James, ed. F.O. Mathiessen and Kenneth B. Murdock, Oxford University Press, London, 1947.

Selected Letters of Henry James, ed. Leon Edel, Rupert Hart-Davis, London, 1956.

Criticism

BOWDEN, EDWIN T.: *The Themes of Henry James*, Yale University Press, New Haven, 1956.

EDEL, LEON: *The Life of Henry James*, 5 vols, Rupert Hart-Davis, London, 1953–72.
(*The Untried Years, 1843–70; The Conquest of London, 1870–83; The Middle Years, 1884–94; The Treacherous Years, 1895–1900; The Master, 1901–16*)
A famous and definitive critical biography.

GARD, ROGER (ED): *Henry James: The Critical Heritage*, Routledge and Kegan Paul, London, 1968.

GOODE, JOHN (ED.): *The Air of Reality: New Essays on Henry James*, Methuen, London, 1972. John Lucas's essay on *Washington Square* is a Marxist interpretation.

KELLEY, CORNELIA PULSIFER: *The Early Development of Henry James*, University of Illinois Press, Urbana, 1965. Interesting on James's development and his relation to Balzac.

POIRIER, RICHARD: *The Comic Sense of Henry James*, Chatto and Windus, London, 1960. A brilliant study of James's early novels including *Washington Square*.

WILLEN, GERALD (ED.): *Washington Square: text and criticism*, Thomas Y. Crowell, New York, 1970. The essays by Leo Gurko and David J. Gordon are particularly useful.

The author of these notes

IAN RICHARDS was born in New Zealand and completed his B.A. in English at the University of Canterbury. Later he took his M.A. in modern literature at Queen Mary College, University of London. He studied for a diploma in Teaching English as a Second Language at the Victoria University of Wellington, New Zealand, and is now living and teaching in Osaka, Japan.

The first 200 titles

64 · List of titles

		Series number
SIR WALTER SCOTT	Ivanhoe	(58)
	Quentin Durward	(54)
	The Heart of Midlothian	(141)
	Waverley	(122)
PETER SHAFFER	The Royal Hunt of the Sun	(170)
WILLIAM SHAKESPEARE	A Midsummer Night's Dream	(26)
	Antony and Cleopatra	(82)
	As You Like It	(108)
	Coriolanus	(35)
	Cymbeline	(93)
	Hamlet	(84)
	Henry IV Part I	(83)
	Henry IV Part II	(140)
	Henry V	(40)
	Julius Caesar	(13)
	King Lear	(18)
	Love's Labour's Lost	(72)
	Macbeth	(4)
	Measure for Measure	(33)
	Much Ado About Nothing	(73)
	Othello	(34)
	Richard II	(41)
	Richard III	(119)
	Romeo and Juliet	(64)
	Sonnets	(181)
	The Merchant of Venice	(107)
	The Taming of the Shrew	(118)
	The Tempest	(22)
	The Winter's Tale	(65)
	Troilus and Cressida	(47)
	Twelfth Night	(42)
GEORGE BERNARD SHAW	Androcles and the Lion	(56)
	Arms and the Man	(12)
	Caesar and Cleopatra	(57)
	Major Barbara	(195)
	Pygmalion	(5)
RICHARD BRINSLEY SHERIDAN	The School for Scandal	(55)
	The Rivals	(104)
WOLE SOYINKA	The Lion and the Jewel	(158)
	The Road	(133)
	Three Short Plays	(172)
JOHN STEINBECK	Of Mice and Men	(23)
	The Grapes of Wrath	(7)
	The Pearl	(99)
ROBERT LOUIS STEVENSON	Kidnapped	(90)
	Treasure Island	(48)
	Dr Jekyll and Mr Hyde	(132)
JONATHAN SWIFT	Gulliver's Travels	(61)
JOHN MILLINGTON SYNGE	The Playboy of the Western World	(111)
W. M. THACKERAY	Vanity Fair	(19)
DYLAN THOMAS	Under Milk Wood	(197)
J. R. R. TOLKIEN	The Hobbit	(121)
MARK TWAIN	Huckleberry Finn	(49)
	Tom Sawyer	(76)
VOLTAIRE	Candide	(81)
EVELYN WAUGH	Decline and Fall	(178)
JOHN WEBSTER	The Duchess of Malfi	(171)
	The White Devil	(176)
H. G. WELLS	The History of Mr Polly	(86)
	The Invisible Man	(52)
	The War of the Worlds	(103)
ARNOLD WESKER	Chips with Everything	(184)
	Roots	(164)
PATRICK WHITE	Voss	(190)
OSCAR WILDE	The Importance of Being Earnest	(75)
TENNESSEE WILLIAMS	The Glass Menagerie	(187)
VIRGINIA WOOLF	To the Lighthouse	(162)
WILLIAM WORDSWORTH	Selected Poems	(196)